MW00364549

Betty Crocker

party
food

100 Recipes for the Way You Really Cook

JG PRESS

Copyright © 2007 by General Mills, Minneapolis, MN. All rights reserved.

Published by World Publications Group, Inc., 140 Laurel Street, East Bridgewater, MA 02333, www.wrldpub.net

No part of this publication may be reproduced, stored in a retrieval system or transmitted in any form or by any means, electronic, mechanical, photocopying, recording, scanning or otherwise, except as permitted under Sections 107 or 108 of the 1976 United States Copyright Act, without either the prior written permission of the Publisher, or authorization through payment of the appropriate per-copy fee to the Copyright Clearance Center, 222 Rosewood Drive, Danvers, MA 01923, (978) 750-8400, fax (978) 646-8600. Requests to the Publisher for permission should be addressed to the Permissions Department, John Wiley & Sons, Inc., 111 River Street, Hoboken, NJ 07030, (201) 748-6011, fax (201) 748-6008, or online at http://wiley.com/go/permissions.

Limit of Liability/Disclaimer of Warranty: While the publisher and author have used their best efforts in preparing this book, they make no representations or warranties with respect to the accuracy or completeness of the contents of this book and specifically disclaim any implied warranties of merchantability or fitness for a particular purpose. No warranty may be created or extended by sales representatives or written sales materials. The advice and strategies contained herein may not be suitable for your situation. You should consult with a professional where appropriate. Neither the publisher nor author shall be liable for any loss of profit or any other commercial damages, including but not limited to special, incidental, consequential, or other damages.

Library of Congress Cataloging-in-Publication Data is available upon request.

ISBN: 978-1-57215-698-2 (cloth); 978-1-57215-732-3 (cloth)

Manufactured in China

10 9 8 7 6 5 4 3 2 1

Wiley Anniversary Logo: Richard J. Pacifico

Cover photo: Margarita Shrimp Cocktail (page 102)

Our Betty Crocker Kitchens seal guarantees success in your kitchen. Every recipe has been tested in America's Most Trusted Kitchens™ to meet our high standards of reliability, easy preparation and great taste.

Dear Friends,

Are friends coming over? Don't worry—having a get-together just got a whole lot easier. We've compiled our favorite party foods that are sure to please. They taste great and you can prepare them in no time!

You'll find our crowd-pleasing dips like Asiago and Sun-dried Tomato Dip and Orange Yogurt Fruit Dip. Our Crunchy Munchies chapter offers perfect snacks for after school, during work or anytime—not just party time. Do you love chicken wings? Firecracker Chicken Wings make the perfect addition to any Super Bowl party or family picnic. And don't forget desserts that people can pick up and serve themselves!

Anytime is party time with Betty in the kitchen. So fix yourself a plate, toast your friends and family, turn up the music and have a great time!

Warmly,

Betty Crocker

contents

Party Prep

Go ahead ... ask some friends over for an informal party. These great tips will help you feed them without a lot of fuss.

Instant Party List: Supplies

It's 2 hours before your party, you're standing at the local club store, shopping cart at the ready—now what? Run down this checklist for all you need to serve food and drinks with little to no cleanup.

- **Party plates** — Buy both small 7-inch cocktail-size plates and large 12-inch buffet-size ones. Plastic or heavy-duty coated paper ones are the sturdiest.

- **Cups** — Stock up on the 16-ounce drink cups (look for the colorful, sturdier plastic ones) and 9-ounce hot cups for coffee and even soups. Don't forget to pick up ice!

- **Bright paper napkins** — Pick up some small cocktail napkins, plus the largest dinner-size ones you can find.

- **"Silverware"** — Buy the knives, forks, and spoons that come in colorful durable plastic; they're washable and reusable.

- **Party picks** — Toothpicks work fine, but the colorful longer plastic party picks are more fun —and sturdier!

- **Serving trays** — Party stores carry sturdy platters in clear plastic and silver or gold aluminum foil. They're perfect platters, plus they're reusable!

- **Wicker baskets** — A couple of shallow wicker baskets (about 10 inches and 15 inches) come in handy for serving breads, fresh vegetables, berries, grapes and cookies.

- **Packet of colorful plastic straws** — Get them in fun neon colors or with stripes.

Instant Party List: Food

Low on time? Fill your shopping basket with foods that short-cut cooking times, yet still say "homemade" and taste great!

- **From the Dairy Case:** You'll find yogurt (plain or fruit-flavored) for dips and dessert toppings; sour cream and cream cheese for dips (the original full-fat ones whip up the best); crème fraîche for topping fresh fruits; a tub of whipped butter for easy spreading; hummus; fresh pastas that cook in mere minutes.

- **From the Cheese Counter:** Choose a tub of cream cheese for a fast sandwich spread (plain or flavored); crumbled Roquefort, Gorgonzola, or Maytag blue cheese and shredded sharp Cheddar, provolone, or mozzarella for salads. For the cheese tray, try a selection of an herbed chèvre (goat cheese), a wedge of English Cheddar, a small round gouda, a piece of Brie, and some French triple creme (Brillat Savarin, St. André, Explorateur).

- **From the Deli & Prepared Food Counter:** Look for pre-sliced pepperoni; fresh-sliced meats (smoked turkey, roast beef, honey-glazed ham), a wedge of pâté; pickled mushrooms, knishes (potato, spinach or mushroom); sliced smoked salmon; Tabbouleh or couscous.

- **From the Salad Bar:** Cut-up ingredients can be tossed into salads or soups. Or buy ready-made salads, such as new potato, rotini or macaroni salad and just add ham to turn them into supper.

- **From the Grocer's Aisles:** Look for spaghetti sauces, such as roasted garlic, tomato and basil, even vodka; roasted red peppers and pesto in jars; quality vinegars, such as red wine, balsamic or raspberry; extra virgin olive oil with garlic or pepper; rye and pumpernickel breads; bagel chips; flatbreads flavored with cracked peppercorns and spices or rosemary and sea salt; bread sticks flavored with Parmesan or sun-dried tomatoes and oregano.

Seven Last-Minute Dips

Pressed for time? Whip up one of these dips. Serve with fresh cut vegetables, taco chips, pita bread wedges or long thin bread sticks.

- **Dressed-Up Hummus:** Into purchased hummus, stir some chopped roasted red peppers, a little chopped onion and a splash of fresh lemon juice. Garnish with fresh chopped parsley and serve with pita wedges. (Tip: To spice up hummus, add a dash of cumin.)

- **Sun-dried Tomato Dip:** Combine 8 ounces cream cheese (softened) + 1 cup sour cream + $1/4$ cup minced scallions + 3 tablespoons chopped sun-dried tomatoes (use the dried ones, let stand in boiling water a few minutes, then drain and chop).

- **Fast Salsa Dip:** 8 ounces cream cheese (softened) + 1 cup chunky-style salsa + 2 tablespoons minced onion. Serve with taco chips.

- **Yogurt Cucumber Dip:** 1 cup plain yogurt (don't use non-fat) + 3 tablespoons finely chopped cucumber + 1 tablespoon fresh snipped dill. Serve with pita bread wedges.

- **Blue Cheese Dip:** 8 ounces cream cheese (softened) + 1 cup sour cream + 4 ounces blue cheese (crumbled).

- **Salmon Dip:** 8 ounces cream cheese (softened) + 1 cup sour cream + 8 ounces smoked salmon (flaked and mashed) + a dash of hot pepper sauce.

- **Hot Spinach Dip:** 8 ounces cream cheese (softened) + 1 cup sour cream + one 9-ounce package frozen spinach (thawed and squeezed to drain) + 2 tablespoons minced onion + the juice of a fresh lemon. Mix together and warm in the microwave on High for 3 minutes or until hot, stirring a couple of times.

Party Wraps

Here's the perfect party fare: quick sandwich roll-ups, made on flour tortillas and filled with items you can grab at the grocery store. Buy tortillas in different colors and flavors (like dark-colored whole wheat, red tomato and green spinach). Pick one of the ideas here, roll up tightly, then cut wraps diagonally into one-inch pieces. Place cut-side-up on a platter—and the party's on!

- **Ham & Brie Roll-Up:** Spread a flour tortilla with a mixture of half mayonnaise and half Dijon mustard. Layer on 3 thin slices of ham and top with thin slices of peppered Brie. Sprinkle with fresh snipped dill.

- **Spinach & Cheese:** Spread whipped cream cheese and chives on a green spinach tortilla, and cover with torn up fresh spinach leaves. Top with some chopped roasted red peppers from a jar.

- **Chicken Caesar:** Spread a flour tortilla with bottled Caesar dressing and sprinkle with shredded romaine lettuce and sliced scallions. Add thin slices of smoked cooked chicken and shredded Parmesan. Sprinkle with chopped hard-cooked egg if you like.

- **Salami & Pesto:** Spread a spinach tortilla with store-bought pesto. Cover with thin slices of Genoa salami, minced red onion and a few strips of roasted red peppers from a jar.

Small Bites From Around the World

Serving tiny tastes of food on small plates to enjoy with drinks is a worldwide tradition. (In America, it's the familiar cocktail hour.) Stick with one country or mix and match. However you do it, the best part of serving these small bites is you can buy everything in advance!

- **From Italy: Antipasto ("before the meal")**—Fill a platter with cold roasted or grilled vegetables, such as peppers, onions, eggplant and zucchini, and an assortment of olives. Buy a trio of Italian cheeses, like a chunk of Parmesan, a wedge of Gorgonzola, and some fontina. Pick up a selection of cured sliced meats, such as salami, prosciutto and a stick of pepperoni. Fill a pitcher with some long crispy bread sticks, and finish with fresh grapes.

- **From Spain: Tapas ("covered")**—In Spain, **tapas** are tiny morsels eaten from small plates with drinks, often at a bar, before the main meal. Some say the name **tapas** comes from a tradition of covering a drink with a piece of bread to protect it; it became popular to top this bread with a snack. To make your own, top sliced baguette with **chorizo a la plancha**—the Spanish spicy pork sausage—cooked fast on a very hot griddle or skillet. Boil up some jumbo shrimp in the shell and let your guests do the shelling before eating, as in Spain. Round out the meal with sliced cured Serrano ham, a wedge of Manchego cheese and some little red piquillo peppers.

- **From the Middle East: Meze ("taste, relish")**—This custom spread from Iran to Greece and North Africa. In the Muslim countries, meze is often part of the main meal, but in Greece and the Balkans, it's eaten while drinking and especially while gossiping. Popular offerings include **tzatziki** (cucumber and yogurt dip), hummus, tabbouleh (pick it up ready-made at the store), falafel, stuffed grape leaves, lamb or beef kabobs for grilling, feta cheese and plenty of olives.

Beer-Lover's Peanuts

Southwestern Spiced Party Nuts

Hot and Spicy Peanuts

Ginger-Spiced Almonds

Pizza Nuts

Honey-Cardamom Mixed Nuts

Almond Caramel Corn

Plantain Chips

Baked Pita Chips

Chex® Party Mix

Soy Nut Snack Mix

Roasted Sesame and Honey Snack Mix

Savory Snacktime Mix

Tropical Honey Snack Mix

Chili and Garlic Snack Mix

Honey-Spice Pretzels

Nachos

1

crunchy munchies

Beer-Lover's Peanuts

Prep Time: 7 min ▪ Start to Finish: 7 min ▪ 16 Servings (¼ cup each)

4 teaspoons vegetable oil
1 tablespoon Cajun seasoning
½ teaspoon ground red pepper (cayenne)
4 cups lightly salted dry-roasted peanuts

1 Heat oil in 12-inch skillet over medium heat. Stir in Cajun seasoning and red pepper.

2 Stir in peanuts. Cook about 2 minutes, stirring constantly, until peanuts are evenly coated and hot. Cool slightly. Serve warm or cool. Store tightly covered up to 3 weeks.

1 Serving: Calories 220 (Calories from Fat 170); Total Fat 19g (Saturated Fat 3g); Cholesterol 0mg; Sodium 130mg; Total Carbohydrate 7g (Dietary Fiber 3g); Protein 10g

Southwestern Spiced Party Nuts

Prep Time: 10 min ▪ Start to Finish: 20 min ▪ 9 Servings (¼ cup each)

1 can (9.5 to 11.5 oz) salted mixed nuts
1 tablespoon butter or margarine, melted
2 teaspoons chili powder
½ teaspoon garlic powder
½ teaspoon onion powder
¼ teaspoon ground cinnamon
¼ teaspoon ground red pepper (cayenne)
2 tablespoons sugar

1 Heat oven to 300°F.

2 In medium bowl, mix nuts and butter until nuts are coated. In small bowl, mix remaining ingredients except sugar; sprinkle over nuts. Stir until nuts are completely coated. Spread in single layer in 15×10×1-inch pan.

3 Bake uncovered about 10 minutes or until nuts are toasted. Return to medium bowl.

4 While nuts are still hot, sprinkle with sugar and toss to coat. Serve warm, or cool completely, about 1 hour. Store in airtight container at room temperature up to 3 weeks.

¼ **Cup:** Calories 250 (Calories from Fat 180); Total Fat 21g (Saturated Fat 3.5g); Cholesterol 0mg; Sodium 240mg; Total Carbohydrate 11g (Dietary Fiber 3g); Protein 6g

Hot and Spicy Peanuts

Prep Time: 5 min   Start to Finish: 30 min   16 Servings (2 tablespoons each)

2 teaspoons vegetable oil
2 cloves garlic, crushed
2 cups unsalted dry-roasted peanuts
2 teaspoons chili powder
1/2 teaspoon salt

1 Heat oil in 8-inch skillet over medium heat. Cook garlic in oil, stirring occasionally, until garlic is golden brown; remove garlic and discard.

2 Stir peanuts and chili powder into skillet. Cook over medium heat about 2 minutes, stirring occasionally, until peanuts are warm; drain on paper towels.

3 Sprinkle salt over peanuts. Cool completely. Store in tightly covered container at room temperature.

Be a party nut—make these way ahead, as much as a month.
   Just seal them in an airtight container—nuts whenever you want!

1 Serving: Calories 225 (Calories from Fat 90); Total Fat 10g (Saturated Fat 3g); Cholesterol 0mg; Sodium 160mg; Total Carbohydrate 4g (Dietary Fiber 3g); Protein 10g

Ginger-Spiced Almonds

Prep Time: 30 min   Start to Finish: 2 hrs 5 min   32 Servings (¼ cup each)

5 cups blanched whole almonds
1 cup sugar
1 tablespoon grated gingerroot
1 ½ teaspoons garlic salt
½ teaspoon dry mustard
½ teaspoon onion powder
2 egg whites
⅓ cup butter or margarine, cut into pieces

1 Heat oven to 325°F. In 15×10×1-inch pan, spread almonds. Bake 25 to 30 minutes, stirring occasionally, until lightly toasted.

2 Meanwhile, in small bowl, mix remaining ingredients except egg whites and butter; set aside. In large bowl, beat egg whites with electric mixer on high speed until soft peaks form. Continue beating, gradually adding sugar mixture. Fold in almonds.

3 Place butter in same pan. Place in oven 3 to 5 minutes or until butter is melted. Spread almond mixture over butter. Bake 30 to 35 minutes, stirring every 10 minutes, until almonds are brown and no butter remains. Cool completely, about 1 hour. Store in airtight container.

Check the bulk-foods section of the grocery store for the nuts to make this recipe; it's often cheaper to buy the nuts in bulk rather than in packages.

1 Serving: Calories 180 (Calories from Fat 120); Total Fat 13g (Saturated Fat 2g); Cholesterol 5mg; Sodium 60mg; Total Carbohydrate 11g (Dietary Fiber 3g); Protein 5g

Pizza Nuts

Prep Time: 7 min ▪ Start to Finish: 17 min ▪ 16 Servings (¹/₄ cup each)

4 teaspoons vegetable oil
1 tablespoon pizza seasoning
¹/₂ teaspoon ground red pepper (cayenne)
4 cups lightly salted dry-roasted peanuts

1 Heat oil in 12-inch skillet over medium heat. Stir in pizza seasoning and red pepper.

2 Stir in peanuts. Cook about 2 minutes, stirring constantly, until peanuts are evenly coated and hot. Cool slightly. Serve warm or cool. Store tightly covered up to 3 weeks.

1 Serving: Calories 220 (Calories from Fat 170); Total Fat 19g (Saturated Fat 3g); Cholesterol 0mg; Sodium 125mg; Total Carbohydrate 7g (Dietary Fiber 3g); Protein 10g

Changes are OK—you can use chili powder instead of pizza seasoning; if you don't have ground red pepper on hand, use ¹/₂ teaspoon red pepper sauce.

Honey-Cardamom Mixed Nuts

Prep Time: 10 min ▪ Start to Finish: 55 min ▪ 24 Servings (2 tablespoons each)

$1/4$ cup honey

2 tablespoons butter or margarine, melted

$3/4$ teaspoon ground cardamom

$1/2$ teaspoon salt

$1/2$ teaspoon ground cinnamon

$1/4$ teaspoon ground cloves

$1/4$ teaspoon ground ginger

2 containers (10 oz each) deluxe salted mixed nuts without peanuts

1 Heat oven to 275°F. Spray jelly roll pan, $15^{1}/_{2} \times 10^{1}/_{2} \times 1$ inch, with cooking spray. Mix all ingredients except nuts in large bowl. Add nuts; stir to coat.

2 Spread nuts in pan. Bake 45 minutes, stirring every 15 minutes. Cool in pan, stirring occasionally.

Go nuts—you can use a combination of whatever salted nuts you want. Almonds and cashews are especially elegant and make a great crunchy duo for this mix.

1 Serving: Calories 175 (Calories from Fat 125); Total Fat 14g (Saturated Fat 3g); Cholesterol 5mg; Sodium 220mg; Total Carbohydrate 8g (Dietary Fiber 1g); Protein 4g

Almond Caramel Corn

Prep Time: 20 min   Start to Finish: 1 hr 50 min   About 30 Servings (¹/₂ cup each)

12 cups popped popcorn
3 cups unblanched whole almonds
1 cup packed brown sugar
¹/₂ cup butter or margarine
¹/₄ cup light corn syrup
¹/₂ teaspoon salt
¹/₂ teaspoon baking soda

1 Heat oven to 200°F. Place popcorn and almonds in very large roasting pan or divide popcorn mixture between 2 ungreased rectangular pans, 13×9×2 inches.

2 Heat brown sugar, butter, corn syrup and salt in 2-quart saucepan over medium heat, stirring occasionally, until bubbly around edges. Continue cooking 5 minutes without stirring; remove from heat. Stir in baking soda until foamy.

3 Pour sugar mixture over popcorn; toss until evenly coated. Bake 1 hour, stirring every 15 minutes. Spread on aluminum foil or cooking parchment paper. Cool completely, about 30 minutes. Store tightly covered.

1 Serving: Calories 170 (Calories from Fat 110); Total Fat 12g (Saturated Fat 3g); Cholesterol 10mg; Sodium 90mg; Total Carbohydrate 15g (Dietary Fiber 2g); Protein 3g

Plantain Chips

Prep Time: 30 min ▪ Start to Finish: 30 min ▪ About 4 Servings (½ cup each)

Vegetable oil for deep-frying
2 large green plantains, peeled and cut into ¼-inch slices (4 cups)
½ teaspoon salt
½ teaspoon black peppercorns, crushed
Juice of 1 medium lime (2 tablespoons)

1 Heat oil (2 to 3 inches deep) in wok or Dutch oven over medium-high heat until thermometer inserted in oil reads 350°F.

2 Carefully place about half of the plantain slices in hot oil and fry 4 to 5 minutes, turning occasionally, until golden brown. Remove with slotted spoon; drain on paper towels. Repeat with remaining plantains.

3 Place fried chips in medium bowl. Add salt and pepper; toss gently. Drizzle with lime juice; toss gently.

A plantain may look like a banana, but you can't peel it like one. The best way to prepare it is to wash the plantain first, then cut it crosswise into several pieces. For each piece, cut through the peel lengthwise, then remove the peel from around the flesh.

1 Serving: Calories 190 (Calories from Fat 35); Total Fat 4g (Saturated Fat 1g); Cholesterol 0mg; Sodium 300mg; Total Carbohydrate 40g (Dietary Fiber 3g); Protein 1g

Baked Pita Chips

Prep Time: 15 min   Start to Finish: 15 min   8 Servings (8 chips each)

4 whole wheat pita breads (6 inch)

1 Heat oven to 400°F. Split each pita bread around each edge with knife to make 2 rounds. Cut each round into 8 wedges. Place in single layer on 2 ungreased cookie sheets.

2 Bake about 9 minutes or until crisp and light brown; cool. Store in airtight container at room temperature.

1 Serving: Calories 85 (Calories from Fat 10); Total Fat 1g (Saturated Fat 0g); Cholesterol 0mg; Sodium 170mg; Total Carbohydrate 18g (Dietary Fiber 2g); Protein 3g

Chex® Party Mix

Prep Time: 10 min ▪ Start to Finish: 3 hrs 10 min ▪ 24 Servings (1/2 cup each)

6 tablespoons butter or margarine, melted
2 tablespoons Worcestershire sauce
1/2 teaspoon garlic powder
1/2 teaspoon onion powder
1/4 teaspoon red pepper sauce
3 cups Corn Chex® cereal
3 cups Rice Chex® cereal
3 cups Wheat Chex® cereal
1 cup peanuts
1 cup pretzels
1 cup garlic-flavor bite-size bagel chips or regular-size bagel chips, broken into
     1-inch pieces

1 Mix butter, Worcestershire sauce, garlic powder, onion powder and pepper sauce in 5- to 6-quart slow cooker. Gradually stir in remaining ingredients until evenly coated.

2 Cook uncovered on low heat setting 3 to 4 hours, stirring every 30 minutes, until mix is warm and flavors are blended.

3 Turn off cooker. Serve with large serving spoon.

Could it get any better? The world's favorite snack mix in a no-hassle slow cooker—snack on!

1 Serving: Calories 155 (Calories from Fat 65); Total Fat 7g (Saturated Fat 2g); Cholesterol 10mg; Sodium 310mg; Total Carbohydrate 21g (Dietary Fiber 2g); Protein 4g

Soy Nut Snack Mix

Prep Time: 10 min   Start to Finish: 1 hr 10 min   14 Servings (¹/₂ cup each)

2 tablespoons butter or margarine
1 tablespoon Worcestershire sauce
³/₄ teaspoon seasoned salt
¹/₂ teaspoon garlic powder
3 cups Wheat Chex or Multi-Bran Chex® cereal
2 cups Cheerios® cereal
1 cup pretzel nuggets
1 cup salted roasted soy nuts

1 Heat oven to 250°F. In large roasting pan, melt butter in oven. Stir Worcestershire sauce, seasoned salt and garlic powder into melted butter. Stir in remaining ingredients until all pieces are coated.

2 Bake 1 hour, stirring every 15 minutes. Spread on paper towels to cool. Store in airtight container.

Just like a whole grain contains all three parts and nutrients of the grain, soy nuts contain all the parts and nutrients of the whole soybean.

1 Serving: Calories 130 (Calories from Fat 35); Total Fat 4g (Saturated Fat 1.5g); Cholesterol 0mg; Sodium 300mg; Total Carbohydrate 19g (Dietary Fiber 3g); Protein 4g

Roasted Sesame and Honey Snack Mix

Prep Time: 10 min ▪ Start to Finish: 1 hr 25 min ▪ 20 Servings (¹/₂ cup each)

3 cups Chex cereal (any variety)
3 cups checkerboard-shaped pretzels
3 cups sesame sticks
1 cup mixed nuts
¹/₄ cup honey
3 tablespoons butter or margarine, melted
2 tablespoons sesame seed, toasted, if desired

1 Heat oven to 275°F. Mix cereal, pretzels, sesame sticks and nuts in ungreased jelly roll pan, 15¹/₂×10¹/₂×1 inch.

2 Mix remaining ingredients. Pour over cereal mixture, stirring until evenly coated.

3 Bake 45 minutes, stirring occasionally. Spread on waxed paper; cool. Store in airtight container up to 1 week.

1 Serving: Calories 210 (Calories from Fat 70); Total Fat 8g (Saturated Fat 2g); Cholesterol 5mg; Sodium 50mg; Total Carbohydrate 32g (Dietary Fiber 2g); Protein 4g

Make this snack mix
when you have the time—you
can store it for up to 1 week in an
airtight container.

Savory Snacktime Mix

Prep Time: 10 min ▪ Start to Finish: 40 min ▪ 15 Servings (½ cup each)

2 cups Cheerios cereal
2 cups Chex cereal (any variety)
2 cups pretzels
1 cup peanuts
¼ cup butter or margarine, melted
1 tablespoon Worcestershire sauce
1 teaspoon paprika
½ teaspoon garlic salt

1 Heat oven to 275°F. Mix cereals, pretzels and peanuts in ungreased rectangular pan, 13×9×2 inches.

2 Mix remaining ingredients. Pour over cereal mixture, stirring until evenly coated.

3 Bake 30 minutes, stirring occasionally; cool. Store in airtight container up to 1 week.

A great snack to keep around the house—just keep it in an airtight container.

1 Serving: Calories 130 (Calories from Fat 70); Total Fat 8g (Saturated Fat 3g); Cholesterol 10mg; Sodium 260mg; Total Carbohydrate 12g (Dietary Fiber 2g); Protein 4g

Tropical Honey Snack Mix

Prep Time: 10 min　Start to Finish: 55 min　15 Servings ($\frac{1}{3}$ cup each)

3 tablespoons butter or margarine
3 tablespoons packed brown sugar
3 tablespoons honey
2 teaspoons ground ginger
$\frac{1}{2}$ teaspoon salt
1 jar (6 to 7 oz) macadamia nuts
2 cups small pretzel twists
$\frac{3}{4}$ cup diced dried pineapple, papaya and mango mix (from 7-oz package)

1 Heat oven to 350°F. Line 15×10×1-inch pan with foil. In 12-inch skillet, melt butter over medium heat. Stir in brown sugar, honey, ginger and salt. Cook about 2 minutes, stirring constantly, until bubbly.

2 Add remaining ingredients. Cook about 1 minute, stirring constantly, until all ingredients are coated. Spread mixture in thin layer in foil-lined pan.

3 Bake 10 to 12 minutes, stirring occasionally, until bubbly and lightly browned. On unlined cookie sheet, spread mixture in thin layer. Cool completely, about 30 minutes. Store in airtight container up to 2 weeks.

1 Serving: Calories 170 (Calories from Fat 100); Total Fat 11g (Saturated Fat 2.5g); Cholesterol 5mg; Sodium 220mg; Total Carbohydrate 16g (Dietary Fiber 2g); Protein 2g

Chili and Garlic Snack Mix

Prep Time: 5 min ▪ Start to Finish: 50 min ▪ 14 Servings (½ cup each)

3 cups Cheerios cereal
3 cups corn chips (broken in half, if desired)
1 cup unsalted peanuts
1 cup thin pretzel sticks
⅓ cup butter or margarine, melted
½ teaspoon chili powder
½ teaspoon garlic powder

1 Heat oven to 300°F. In large bowl, mix cereal, corn chips, peanuts and pretzels. In small bowl, mix remaining ingredients; pour over cereal mixture. Toss until evenly coated. In ungreased 15×10×1-inch pan, spread cereal mixture.

2 Bake uncovered 15 minutes, stirring once. Cool completely, about 30 minutes. Store in airtight container.

1 Serving: Calories 170 (Calories from Fat 110); Total Fat 12g (Saturated Fat 3.5g); Cholesterol 10mg; Sodium 170mg; Total Carbohydrate 12g (Dietary Fiber 2g); Protein 4g

Honey-Spice Pretzels

Prep Time: 10 min ▪ Start to Finish: 18 min ▪ 4 Servings (1 cup each)

4 cups fat-free pretzel sticks
3 tablespoons honey
1 teaspoon onion powder
1 teaspoon chili powder
2 teaspoons margarine, melted

1 Heat oven to 350°F. Line cookie sheet with aluminum foil; spray with cooking spray. Place pretzels in large bowl. Mix remaining ingredients; drizzle over pretzels. Toss until evenly coated. Spread pretzels evenly on cookie sheet.

2 Bake 8 minutes, stirring once. Cool on cookie sheet. Loosen pretzels from foil. Store in airtight container at room temperature.

1 Serving: Calories 225 (Calories from Fat 20); Total Fat 2g (Saturated Fat 1g); Cholesterol 0mg; Sodium 800mg; Total Carbohydrate 50g (Dietary Fiber 2g); Protein 4g

Nachos

Prep Time: 5 min   Start to Finish: 9 min   4 Servings

28 tortilla chips
1 cup shredded Monterey Jack or Cheddar cheese (4 oz)
1/4 cup canned chopped mild green chiles, if desired
1/4 cup salsa

1 Heat oven to 400°F. Line cookie sheet with foil.

2 Place tortilla chips on cookie sheet. Sprinkle with cheese and chiles.

3 Bake about 4 minutes or until cheese is melted. Top with salsa. Serve hot.

1 Serving: Calories 170 (Calories from Fat 110); Total Fat 12g (Saturated Fat 6g); Cholesterol 25mg; Sodium 300mg; Total Carbohydrate 9g (Dietary Fiber 0g); Protein 8g

Crowd-Pleasing Drinks

Colada Cooler Punch

Prep Time: 10 min
Start to Finish: 10 min
24 Servings

2 cans (12 oz each) frozen piña
  colada mix concentrate, thawed
2 cans (12 oz each) frozen white
  grape juice concentrate, thawed
6 cups cold water
12 cups (about 3 liters) lemon-lime
  carbonated beverage
Lemon and lime slices

1. In 4-quart container, stir piña colada and juice concentrates until well mixed. Stir in water; refrigerate.

2. Just before serving, pour piña colada mixture into punch bowl. Add soda pop and lemon and lime slices; gently stir. Pour over ice in glasses.

1 Serving: Calories 160 (Calories from Fat 0);
Total Fat 0g (Saturated Fat 0g); Cholesterol 0mg;
Sodium 15mg; Total Carbohydrate 40g
(Dietary Fiber 0g); Protein 0g

Sangria Blanco

Prep Time: 15 min
Start to Finish: 2 hrs 20 min
8 Servings

1/4 cup sugar
1/2 cup water
2 sticks cinnamon, broken in half
1 cup sparkling water
1 cup apple juice
1/2 cup orange juice
1 bottle (750 ml) Chardonnay or
  nonalcoholic wine if desired
1 medium unpeeled orange, cut in
  half and thinly sliced
1 medium unpeeled eating apple, cut
  into thin wedges
1 medium banana, sliced
Ice cubes

1. Heat sugar, water and cinnamon to boiling in 1-quart saucepan; reduce heat. Simmer uncovered 5 minutes. Cover and refrigerate at least 2 hours but no longer than 1 week.

2. Remove cinnamon sticks from sugar mixture. Mix sugar mixture, sparkling water, apple juice, orange juice and wine in large pitcher. Gently stir in fruit and ice. Serve with several pieces fruit in each glass.

1 Serving: Calories 85 (Calories from Fat 0);
Total Fat 0g (Saturated Fat 0g); Cholesterol 0mg;
Sodium 15mg; Total Carbohydrate 21g
(Dietary Fiber 0g); Protein 0g

Sparkling Raspberry Tea

Prep Time: 5 min
Start to Finish: 5 min
6 Servings (1 cup each)

2 cups cold brewed tea
2 cups chilled raspberry or
    cranberry-raspberry juice
2 cups chilled sparkling water
Raspberries, lime slices or lemon
    slices, if desired
Fresh mint leaves, if desired

1.   In large pitcher, mix tea, juice and
sparkling water.

2.   Serve tea over ice. Garnish with
raspberries and mint leaves.

Make raspberry ice cubes by putting 1 or
    2 fresh raspberries in each section of an ice-
    cube tray. Cover with water and freeze.

Warm Cinnamon Orange Cider

Prep Time: 10 min
Start to Finish: 10 min
8 Servings ($^3/_4$ cup each)

$^1/_2$ bottle (64-oz size) apple cider
    (4 cups)
2 cups orange juice
2 tablespoons red cinnamon candies
$1^1/_2$ teaspoons whole allspice
1 tablespoon plus $1^1/_2$ teaspoons
    honey

1.   Mix all ingredients except honey
in 3-quart saucepan. Heat to boiling;
reduce heat. Cover and simmer
5 minutes.

2.   Remove allspice. Stir in honey.
Serve warm.

To serve hot cider at a party, pour the heated
    cider into a slow cooker. Set the cooker on
    Low heat and let everyone help themselves.

1 Serving: Calories 40 (Calories from Fat 0);
Total Fat 0g (Saturated Fat 0g); Cholesterol 0mg;
Sodium 5mg; Total Carbohydrate 9g
(Dietary Fiber 0g); Protein 0g

1 Serving: Calories 110 (Calories from Fat 0);
Total Fat 0g (Saturated Fat 0g); Cholesterol 0mg;
Sodium 5mg; Total Carbohydrate 28g
(Dietary Fiber 0g); Protein 0g

Orange Yogurt Fruit Dip

Dried Fruit and Cream Cheese Roulade

Gingered Fruit Salsa with Crispy Cinnamon Chips

Tomatillo Dip

Chipotle Black Bean Dip

Hummus

Olive Tapenade

Three-Onion Spread

Roasted Carrot and Herb Spread

Roasted Red Pepper and Garlic Spread with Veggies

Zippy Dill Vegetable Dip

Zesty Corn Dip

Spinach-Artichoke Dip

Chipotle Ranch Dip

Asiago and Sun-Dried Tomato Dip

Bacon, Lettuce and Tomato Dip

Smoked Almond, Cheddar and Bacon Dip

Smoky Bacon and Horseradish Dip

Spicy Sausage Nacho Dip

Hot Crab Dip

2

dips and spreads

Orange Yogurt Fruit Dip

Prep Time: 10 min ▪ Start to Finish: 10 min ▪ 16 Servings

1 package (8 oz) reduced-fat cream cheese (Neufchâtel)
1 container (6 oz) fat-free orange crème yogurt
$1/2$ cup orange marmalade
$1/8$ teaspoon ground nutmeg
2 tablespoons coarsely chopped pecans
Grated orange peel
Ground nutmeg, if desired
Assorted fresh fruit

1 In medium bowl, beat cream cheese with electric mixer on medium speed until creamy. Beat in yogurt, marmalade and $1/8$ teaspoon nutmeg until smooth.

2 Spoon into serving bowl. Top with pecans and orange peel. Sprinkle with nutmeg. Serve with fruit.

1 Serving: Calories 110 (Calories from Fat 40); Total Fat 4g (Saturated Fat 2.5g); Cholesterol 10mg; Sodium 65mg; Total Carbohydrate 15g (Dietary Fiber 0g); Protein 2g

Dried Fruit and Cream Cheese Roulade

Prep Time: 15 min   Start to Finish: 2 hrs 15 min   10 Servings

1 package (8 oz) cream cheese
1 tablespoon red currant or apple jelly
1/4 cup chopped dried Calimyrna figs
1/4 cup chopped dried apricots
2 oz crumbled chèvre (goat) cheese
1/4 cup chopped walnuts
1 tablespoon chopped fresh chives
40 assorted crackers

1 Place cream cheese between 2 sheets of plastic wrap. Roll into 9×6-inch rectangle with rolling pin. Remove top sheet of wrap. Carefully spread jelly over cream cheese. Sprinkle with figs and apricots to within 1/2 inch of edges. Sprinkle with cheese.

2 Using bottom sheet of wrap to help lift and starting at a long side, carefully roll up cheese mixture into a log. Carefully press walnuts into outside of log, rolling slightly to cover all sides. Wrap tightly in plastic wrap. Refrigerate at least 2 hours to set.

3 To serve, place roulade on serving plate. Sprinkle with chives. Serve with crackers.

1 Serving: Calories 170 (Calories from Fat 100); Total Fat 11g (Saturated Fat 5g); Cholesterol 20mg; Sodium 160mg; Total Carbohydrate 14g (Dietary Fiber 1g); Protein 4g

Gingered Fruit Salsa with Crispy Cinnamon Chips

Prep Time: 50 min ▪ Start to Finish: 1 hr 5 min ▪ 24 Servings

1 tablespoon sugar
2 teaspoons ground cinnamon
6 flour tortillas (9 to 10 inch)
3 tablespoons butter or margarine, melted
1 cup finely diced pineapple
1 cup finely diced papaya
1 cup finely diced mango
1/4 cup chopped fresh cilantro
1 tablespoon finely chopped crystallized ginger
1 tablespoon lemon juice
1/8 teaspoon salt

1 Set oven control to broil. Mix sugar and cinnamon. Brush both sides of each tortilla with butter; sprinkle with sugar-cinnamon mixture. Cut each tortilla into 12 wedges.

2 Place tortilla wedges in single layer in 2 ungreased jelly roll pans, 15½×10½×1 inch, or on 2 cookie sheets. Broil 2 to 4 minutes, turning once, until crispy and golden brown. Cool completely.

3 Mix remaining ingredients. Serve salsa with chips.

Use your pizza cutter to easily cut the tortillas into wedges.

1 Serving: Calories 55 (Calories from Fat 20); Total Fat 2g (Saturated Fat 1g); Cholesterol 5mg; Sodium 75mg; Total Carbohydrate 9g (Dietary Fiber 1g); Protein 1g

Tomatillo Dip

Prep Time: 40 min ▪ Start to Finish: 1 hr 40 min ▪ 3 Servings

1/2 cup water
1/4 teaspoon salt
1/8 teaspoon ground cumin
1/8 teaspoon pepper
1-inch fresh Anaheim chile, seeds and ribs removed and coarsely chopped
1/2- to 1-inch fresh hot red jalapeño chile, coarsely chopped, if desired
2 green onions, coarsely chopped
1/2 pound tomatillos (about 6 or 7), husked, washed and quartered
2 tablespoons fresh cilantro leaves, loosely packed

1 Place all ingredients except cilantro in 1-quart saucepan. Cover and cook over medium heat 12 to 15 minutes, stirring occasionally, until tomatillos are soft. Cool 15 minutes.

2 Place in blender or food processor. Add cilantro. Cover and blend at medium-high speed, stopping blender occasionally to scrape sides, until smooth. Refrigerate at least 1 hour or until chilled.

You can substitute 1 large green tomato, chopped, and 1 teaspoon lime juice for the tomatillos.

1 Serving: Calories 20 (Calories from Fat 0); Total Fat 0 (Saturated Fat 0g); Cholesterol 0mg; Sodium 190mg; Total Carbohydrate 5g (Dietary Fiber 1g); Protein 1g

Chipotle Black Bean Dip

Prep Time: 20 min ▪ Start to Finish: 45 min ▪ 15 Servings

2 large dried chipotle chiles
1 cup chunky-style salsa
½ cup jalapeño black bean dip
2 tablespoons chopped fresh cilantro
1 cup shredded Colby–Monterey Jack cheese blend (4 oz)
2 medium green onions, chopped (2 tablespoons)
Sweet red cherry chili half, if desired
Tortilla chips, if desired

1 Heat oven to 350°F. Cover chiles with boiling water; let stand 10 minutes. Drain chiles and remove seeds. Chop chiles.

2 Mix chiles, salsa and bean dip; stir in cilantro. (If making ahead, cover and refrigerate up to 24 hours.) Spoon into shallow 1-quart ovenproof serving dish. Sprinkle with cheese.

3 Bake about 15 minutes or until mixture is hot and cheese is melted. Sprinkle with onions. Garnish with chili half. Serve with tortilla chips.

1 Serving: Calories 45 (Calories from Fat 30); Total Fat 3g (Saturated Fat 2g); Cholesterol 10mg; Sodium 150mg; Total Carbohydrate 2g (Dietary Fiber 1g); Protein 2g

Hummus

Prep Time: 5 min ▪ Start to Finish: 5 min ▪ 16 Servings

1 can (15 to 16 oz) garbanzo beans, drained and $\frac{1}{3}$ cup liquid reserved
3 tablespoons lemon juice
$\frac{1}{2}$ cup sesame seed
1 clove garlic, crushed
1 teaspoon salt
Chopped fresh parsley
Raw vegetables or crackers, if desired

1 Place beans, reserved bean liquid, lemon juice, sesame seed, garlic and salt in blender or food processor. Cover and blend on high speed, stopping blender occasionally to scrape sides if necessary, until uniform consistency.

2 Spoon dip into serving dish. Sprinkle with parsley. Serve with vegetables.

1 Serving: Calories 65 (Calories from Fat 25); Total Fat 3g (Saturated Fat 0g); Cholesterol 0mg; Sodium 190mg; Total Carbohydrate 8g (Dietary Fiber 3g); Protein 4g

Olive Tapenade

Prep Time: 10 min ▪ Start to Finish: 10 min ▪ 14 Servings

1½ cups pitted ripe olives
¼ cup chopped walnuts
3 tablespoons olive or vegetable oil
3 tablespoons capers, drained
1½ teaspoons fresh rosemary leaves
1 teaspoon Italian seasoning
2 cloves garlic
Chopped red bell pepper
Assorted crackers, if desired

1 Place all ingredients except bell pepper and crackers in food processor or blender. Cover and process, using quick on-and-off motions, until slightly coarse.

2 Spoon into serving dish; sprinkle with bell pepper. Serve with crackers.

For a more authentic flavor, use pitted kalamata olives instead of ripe olives.

1 Serving: Calories 60 (Calories from Fat 55); Total Fat 6g (Saturated Fat 1g); Cholesterol 0mg; Sodium 190mg; Total Carbohydrate 2g (Dietary Fiber 1g); Protein 1g

Three-Onion Spread

Prep Time: 15 min   Start to Finish: 15 min   12 Servings

2 tablespoons olive or vegetable oil
1 large sweet onion (such as Walla Walla or Maui), chopped (1 cup)
1 large red onion, chopped (1 cup)
1 tablespoon chopped fresh parsley
1 tub (8 oz) soft cream cheese with chives and onion
Assorted crackers and breadsticks, if desired

1 Heat oil in 10-inch skillet over medium heat. Cook onions in oil about 5 minutes, stirring occasionally, until tender.

2 Stir in parsley and cream cheese until smooth. Spoon into serving dish. Serve warm or cold with crackers.

1 Serving: Calories 90 (Calories from Fat 70); Total Fat 8g (Saturated Fat 4g); Cholesterol 20mg; Sodium 55mg; Total Carbohydrate 3g (Dietary Fiber 0g); Protein 2g

Roasted Carrot and Herb Spread

Prep Time: 10 min ▪ Start to Finish: 55 min ▪ 20 Servings

2 pounds baby-cut carrots
1 large sweet potato, peeled and cut into 1-inch pieces
1 medium onion, cut into 8 wedges and separated
1/4 cup olive or vegetable oil
2 tablespoons chopped fresh or 1 teaspoon dried thyme leaves
2 cloves garlic, finely chopped
3/4 teaspoon salt
1/4 teaspoon freshly ground pepper
Baguette slices or crackers, if desired

1 Heat oven to 350°F. Spray jelly roll pan, 15½×10½×1 inch, with cooking spray.

2 Place carrots, sweet potato and onion in pan. Drizzle with oil. Sprinkle with thyme, garlic, salt and pepper. Stir to coat. Bake uncovered 35 to 45 minutes, stirring occasionally, until vegetables are tender.

3 Place vegetable mixture in food processor. Cover and process until blended. Spoon into serving bowl. Serve warm, or cover and refrigerate until serving time. Serve with baguette slices.

1 Serving: Calories 40 (Calories from Fat 20); Total Fat 2g (Saturated Fat 0g); Cholesterol 0mg; Sodium 100mg; Total Carbohydrate 8g (Dietary Fiber 2g); Protein 0g

Roasted Red Pepper and Garlic Spread with Veggies

Prep Time: 30 min   Start to Finish: 30 min   16 Servings

1 package (3 oz) cream cheese, softened
1 container (6.5 oz) garlic-and-herbs spreadable cheese
1/3 cup grated Parmesan cheese
1/4 cup finely chopped drained roasted red bell peppers (from 7-oz jar)
1 package (8 oz) cream cheese, softened
Finely chopped fresh parsley
Assorted raw vegetables and crackers, if desired

1 Mix 3 ounces cream cheese, the spreadable cheese, Parmesan cheese and bell peppers until blended. Shape mixture into cone shape; place upright on serving plate.

2 Frost cone with 8 ounces cream cheese; sprinkle with parsley. Serve spread with vegetables and crackers.

Save some time by cutting the vegetables one day ahead. Just wrap them tightly with plastic wrap and stash in the refrigerator.

1 Serving: Calories 90 (Calories from Fat 70); Total Fat 8g (Saturated Fat 5g); Cholesterol 25mg; Sodium 190mg; Total Carbohydrate 2g (Dietary Fiber 0g); Protein 3g

Zippy Dill Vegetable Dip

Prep Time: 20 min ▪ Start to Finish: 20 min ▪ 8 Servings

¹/₂ package (0.7-oz size) dill dip mix (about 4 teaspoons)
1 container (8 oz) sour cream
2 tablespoons finely sliced chives
1 tablespoon lemon juice
1 cup ready-to-eat baby-cut carrots
2 cups broccoli florets
¹/₂ pint (1 cup) cherry or grape tomatoes
1 medium cucumber, cut into ¹/₄-inch slices (2 cups)

1 In medium bowl, mix dip mix (dry), sour cream, chives and lemon juice.

2 On serving platter, arrange carrots, broccoli, tomatoes and cucumber slices. Serve with dip.

1 Serving: Calories 80 (Calories from Fat 45); Total Fat 5g (Saturated Fat 2.5g); Cholesterol 10mg; Sodium 220mg; Total Carbohydrate 6g (Dietary Fiber 2g); Protein 2g

For an easy way to slice chives, snip them with your kitchen scissors.

Zesty Corn Dip

Prep Time: 10 min ▪ Start to Finish: 1 hr 10 min ▪ 24 Servings

2 packages (8 oz each) cream cheese, softened
1/4 cup lime juice
1 tablespoon ground red chiles or chili powder
1 tablespoon ground cumin
2 tablespoons vegetable oil
1/2 teaspoon salt
Dash of pepper
1 can (7 oz) whole kernel corn, drained
1/4 cup chopped walnuts
1 small onion, chopped (1/4 cup)
Tortilla chips

1 In large bowl, beat cream cheese, lime juice, chiles, cumin, oil, salt and pepper with electric mixer on medium speed until smooth. Stir in corn, walnuts and onion.

2 Refrigerate at least 1 hour. Serve with tortilla chips.

1 Serving: Calories 120 (Calories from Fat 90); Total Fat 10g (Saturated Fat 4.5g); Cholesterol 20mg; Sodium 150mg; Total Carbohydrate 6g (Dietary Fiber 0g); Protein 2g

For a fun serving idea, fill hollowed-out large bell peppers with the dip.

Spinach-Artichoke Dip

Prep Time: 10 min ▪ Start to Finish: 1 hr 25 min ▪ 24 Servings

1 cup mayonnaise or salad dressing
1 cup freshly grated Parmesan cheese
1 can (about 14 oz) artichoke hearts, drained, coarsely chopped
1 box (10 oz) frozen spinach, thawed, squeezed to drain
$1/2$ cup chopped red bell pepper
$1/4$ cup shredded Monterey Jack or mozzarella cheese (1 oz)
Toasted French baguette slices, assorted crackers or pita chips

1 Spray inside of 1- to $2^1/_2$-quart slow cooker with cooking spray. In medium bowl, mix mayonnaise and Parmesan cheese. Stir in artichoke hearts, spinach and bell pepper. Spoon into slow cooker. Sprinkle with Monterey Jack cheese.

2 Cover and cook on low heat setting 1 hour to 1 hour 15 minutes or until cheese is melted. Serve warm with baguette slices. Dip will hold up to 2 hours.

1 Serving: Calories 350 (Calories from Fat 110); Total Fat 12g (Saturated Fat 3g); Cholesterol 10mg; Sodium 750mg; Total Carbohydrate 51g (Dietary Fiber 4g); Protein 11g

Want to make pita chips? Broil buttered wedges of pita bread 4 to 6 inches from heat for 2 to 4 minutes, turning once.

Chipotle Ranch Dip

Prep Time: 5 min   Start to Finish: 5 min   12 Servings

1½ cups ranch dressing
2 chipotle chiles in adobo sauce (from 7-oz can), drained
Raw vegetables, if desired

1 Place dressing and chiles in blender. Cover and blend until smooth.

2 Serve dip immediately with vegetables, or cover and refrigerate up to 1 week.

You can substitute a 4.5-ounce can of chopped green chiles for the chipotle chiles, if you like.

1 Serving: Calories 140 (Calories from Fat 125); Total Fat 14g (Saturated Fat 1g); Cholesterol 10mg; Sodium 360mg; Total Carbohydrate 2g (Dietary Fiber 0g); Protein 1g

Asiago and Sun-Dried Tomato Dip

Prep Time: 15 min ▪ Start to Finish: 35 min ▪ 40 Servings

$1/3$ cup sun-dried tomatoes (not in oil)
1 cup boiling water
1 package (8 oz) cream cheese, softened
1 cup finely shredded Asiago cheese (4 oz)
8 medium green onions, thinly sliced ($1/2$ cup)
1 cup chopped mushrooms (3 oz)
$1^1/_2$ cups sour cream
13 dozen assorted crackers

1 Mix tomatoes and water; let stand 10 minutes. Drain thoroughly and chop.

2 Heat chopped tomatoes and remaining ingredients except crackers in 2-quart saucepan over medium-low heat, stirring frequently, until cream cheese is melted.

3 Spray inside of $1^1/_2$-quart slow cooker with cooking spray. Transfer tomato mixture to slow cooker. Serve dip with crackers. Dip will hold on low heat setting up to 2 hours. Scrape down side of cooker with rubber spatula occasionally to help prevent edge of dip from scorching.

Because the cheeses are rich, the dip may start to separate, and little puddles could appear on the surface. Just stir the dip occasionally, and it will look as good as new.

1 Serving: Calories 120 (Calories from Fat 70); Total Fat 8g (Saturated Fat 4g); Cholesterol 15mg; Sodium 190mg; Total Carbohydrate 9g (Dietary Fiber 0g); Protein 3g

Bacon, Lettuce and Tomato Dip

Prep Time: 30 min ▪ Start to Finish: 30 min ▪ 16 Servings

1 cup sour cream with chives and onions
$1/4$ cup mayonnaise or salad dressing
$1/2$ cup crumbled cooked bacon (about 8 slices)
$1^{1}/_{2}$ cups shredded romaine lettuce
$1/2$ cup chopped plum (Roma) tomatoes
1 tablespoon chopped fresh chives
32 slices ($1/4$-inch-thick) baguette-style French bread (from 10-oz loaf)

1 Mix sour cream and mayonnaise in small bowl until blended. Stir in bacon.

2 Arrange lettuce in shallow bowl or on small platter. Spoon sour cream mixture over lettuce. Top with tomatoes; sprinkle with chives. Serve with baguette slices.

This dip can be prepared up to 24 hours in advance; just refrigerate the components separately and assemble it right before serving.

1 Serving: Calories 120 (Calories from Fat 65); Total Fat 7g (Saturated Fat 3g); Cholesterol 15mg; Sodium 180mg; Total Carbohydrate 11g (Dietary Fiber 1g); Protein 3g

Smoked Almond, Cheddar and Bacon Dip

Prep Time: 30 min ▪ Start to Finish: 45 min ▪ 32 Servings

2 packages (8 oz each) cream cheese, cubed
3 jars (5 oz each) process sharp Cheddar cheese spread
$1/2$ cup milk
1 clove garlic, finely chopped
2 medium green onions, thinly sliced (2 tablespoons)
$1/2$ cup coarsely chopped canned smoked whole almonds
4 slices bacon, crisply cooked and crumbled
Assorted raw vegetables or breadsticks, if desired

1 Heat cream cheese, cheese spread, milk and garlic in 2-quart saucepan over medium heat, stirring frequently, until cheese is melted and smooth. Stir in onions and $1/4$ cup of the almonds.

2 Spoon into 1-quart slow cooker to keep warm if desired or into serving bowl. Sprinkle with bacon and remaining $1/4$ cup almonds. Serve with vegetables. Dip will hold in slow cooker on low heat setting up to 2 hours; stir occasionally.

Use your slow cooker as the easiest serving bowl possible.

1 Serving: Calories 105 (Calories from Fat 80); Total Fat 9g (Saturated Fat 5g); Cholesterol 25mg; Sodium 260mg; Total Carbohydrate 2g (Dietary Fiber 0g); Protein 4g

Smoky Bacon and Horseradish Dip

Prep Time: 10 min ▪ Start to Finish: 3 hrs 25 min ▪ 24 Servings

1 clove garlic, finely chopped
1 small onion, finely chopped (¼ cup)
1 package (8 oz) cream cheese, cubed
2 cups shredded Gruyère cheese (8 oz)
1 cup half-and-half
8 slices peppered smoked bacon, crisply cooked and chopped
2 tablespoons cream-style prepared horseradish
⅓ cup chopped fresh Italian parsley
French or herbed bread cubes, if desired
Water crackers, if desired

1 Mix garlic, onion, cream cheese, Gruyère cheese and half-and-half in 1½-quart slow cooker.

2 Cover and cook on low heat setting 2½ to 3 hours or until mixture is hot.

3 Stir in bacon, horseradish and parsley. Cover and cook on high heat setting about 15 minutes or until mixture is hot. Serve with bread cubes or crackers for dipping.

Go ahead and use precooked bacon slices found in the deli section of the supermarket. There's no need to cook; just chop and stir into the mixture.

1 Serving: Calories 95 (Calories from Fat 70); Total Fat 8g (Saturated Fat 5g); Cholesterol 25mg; Sodium 95mg; Total Carbohydrate 3g (Dietary Fiber 0g); Protein 4g

Spicy Sausage Nacho Dip

Prep Time: 20 min   Start to Finish: 4 hrs 20 min   16 Servings

1 ¼ pounds bulk chorizo sausage
⅓ cup finely chopped onion
3 cloves garlic, finely chopped
1 package (16 oz) mild Mexican pasteurized prepared cheese product with
      jalapeño peppers, cut into cubes
1 can (14.5 oz) crushed fire-roasted tomatoes, undrained
¼ cup chopped fresh cilantro
9 oz tortilla chips

1 Cook sausage, onion and garlic in 12-inch skillet over medium-high heat, stirring occasionally, until sausage is no longer pink; drain well.

2 Place chorizo mixture, cheese and tomatoes in 2½- to 3½-quart slow cooker.

3 Cover and cook on Low heat setting 3 to 4 hours, stirring halfway through cooking, until cheese is melted and mixture is hot.

4 Stir in cilantro. Serve with tortilla chips for dipping. Dip will hold on Low heat setting up to 1½ hours; stir occasionally.

1 Serving: Calories 350 (Calories from Fat 240); Total Fat 26g (Saturated Fat 11g); Cholesterol 60mg; Sodium 980mg; Total Carbohydrate 13g (Dietary Fiber 0g); Protein 16g

Hot Crab Dip

Prep Time: 15 min ▪ Start to Finish: 35 min ▪ 20 Servings

1 package (8 oz) cream cheese, softened
4 medium green onions, sliced ($\frac{1}{4}$ cup)
1 clove garlic, finely chopped
$\frac{1}{4}$ cup grated Parmesan cheese
$\frac{1}{4}$ cup mayonnaise or salad dressing
$\frac{1}{4}$ cup dry white wine or apple juice
2 teaspoons sugar
1 teaspoon ground mustard
1 can (6 oz) crabmeat, drained, cartilage removed and flaked
$\frac{1}{3}$ cup sliced almonds
Assorted crackers or sliced fresh vegetables

1 Heat oven to 375°F. In ungreased 1$\frac{1}{2}$-quart casserole or 9-inch glass pie plate, mix cream cheese, onions, garlic, Parmesan cheese, mayonnaise, wine, sugar and mustard. Stir in crabmeat. Sprinkle with almonds.

2 Bake uncovered 15 to 20 minutes or until hot and bubbly. Serve with crackers.

You can use 6 ounces imitation crabmeat, coarsely chopped, instead of the canned crabmeat in this recipe.

1 Serving: Calories 120 (Calories from Fat 80); Total Fat 9g (Saturated Fat 3.5g); Cholesterol 20mg; Sodium 130mg; Total Carbohydrate 5g (Dietary Fiber 0g); Protein 4g

Shrimp Nacho Bites

Spicy Grilled Shrimp

Firecracker Chicken Wings

Caribbean Chicken Wings

Baked Buffalo Wings

Spicy Thai Chicken Wings

Grilled Seasoned Chicken Drummettes

Chipotle Chicken Drummettes

Maple Chicken Drummettes

Quick Chicken Quesadillas

Barbecue Pork Bites

Mini Corn Dogs on a Stick

Southwest Riblets

Grilled Veggies and Steak

Appetizer Meatballs

Baby Burgers

3

hot wings 'n' things

Shrimp Nacho Bites

Prep Time: 15 min ▪ Start to Finish: 15 min ▪ 24 Appetizers

24 large corn tortilla chips
1/2 cup black bean dip (from 9-oz can)
1/4 cup chunky-style salsa
24 cooked peeled deveined medium shrimp (about 1/2 lb)
1 avocado, pitted, peeled and cut into 24 slices
1/2 cup shredded Colby–Monterey Jack cheese blend (2 oz)
24 fresh cilantro leaves, if desired

1 Top each tortilla chip with about 1 teaspoon bean dip, 1/2 teaspoon salsa, 1 shrimp, 1 avocado slice and about 1 teaspoon cheese. Place on cookie sheet.

2 Set oven control to broil. Broil with tops about 5 inches from heat 2 to 3 minutes or just until cheese is melted. Garnish with cilantro leaves. Serve immediately.

1 Appetizer: Calories 40 (Calories from Fat 25); Total Fat 3g (Saturated Fat 1g); Cholesterol 15mg; Sodium 85mg; Total Carbohydrate 2g (Dietary Fiber 1g); Protein 2g

Spicy Grilled Shrimp

Prep Time: 10 min ▪ Start to Finish: 40 min ▪ 20 Servings (1 kabob each)

Coconut Curry Sauce

1 cup canned coconut milk
    (not cream of coconut)
2 teaspoons curry powder
2 teaspoons cornstarch
1 teaspoon honey
1/4 teaspoon salt

Shrimp

60 uncooked peeled deveined
    medium shrimp (about
    2 lb), thawed if frozen
1/4 cup olive or vegetable oil
1 teaspoon red pepper sauce

1 Soak twenty 6-inch wooden skewers in water 30 minutes. Meanwhile, heat coals or gas grill for direct heat.

2 Make sauce: Mix all ingredients in small microwavable bowl. Microwave uncovered on High about 2 minutes, stirring every 30 seconds, until mixture bubbles and thickens.

3 Place shrimp in large bowl. Drizzle with oil and pepper sauce; toss to coat. Thread 3 shrimp on each skewer.

4 Cover and grill kabobs 4 to 6 inches from medium heat 4 to 6 minutes or until shrimp are pink and firm. Serve with sauce.

1 Serving: Calories 60 (Calories from Fat 45); Total Fat 5g (Saturated Fat 2g); Cholesterol 30mg; Sodium 75mg; Total Carbohydrate 2g (Dietary Fiber 0g); Protein 3g

Firecracker Chicken Wings

Prep Time: 35 min ■ Start to Finish: 1 hr 5 min ■ 4 Servings

12 chicken wings (2½ lb)
2 tablespoons chili powder
1½ teaspoons dried oregano leaves
1¼ teaspoons ground red pepper (cayenne)
1 teaspoon garlic salt
1 teaspoon ground cumin
1 teaspoon pepper
Sour cream, if desired

1 Fold tips of chicken wings under opposite ends to form triangles.

2 Place remaining ingredients except sour cream in heavy-duty resealable plastic bag. Seal bag and shake to blend seasonings. Add chicken. Seal bag and shake until chicken is coated with seasonings. Refrigerate at least 30 minutes but no longer than 24 hours.

3 Heat coals or gas grill.

4 Cover and grill chicken 4 to 6 inches from medium heat 20 to 25 minutes, turning after 10 minutes, until juice of chicken is no longer pink when centers of thickest pieces are cut. Serve chicken with sour cream.

The wings can be grilled ahead of time, refrigerated and served cold.

1 Serving: Calories 310 (Calories from Fat 200); Total Fat 22g (Saturated Fat 6g); Cholesterol 90mg; Sodium 160mg; Total Carbohydrate 1g (Dietary Fiber 0g); Protein 27g

Caribbean Chicken Wings

Prep Time: 10 min ▪ Start to Finish: 1 hr 10 min ▪ 24 Appetizers

$1/2$ cup pineapple juice
$1/2$ cup ketchup
$1/4$ cup packed brown sugar
$1/4$ cup teriyaki marinade and sauce
$1/4$ cup honey
2 cloves garlic, finely chopped
2 lb chicken drummettes (about 24)

1 Heat oven to 350°F. Line rectangular pan, 13×9×2 inches, with aluminum foil.

2 Heat all ingredients except chicken to boiling in 1-quart saucepan, stirring occasionally. Place chicken in pan; pour sauce over chicken.

3 Bake uncovered about 1 hour, turning chicken 2 to 3 times, until juice of chicken is no longer pink when centers of thickest pieces are cut.

4 Spray inside of 3$1/2$-quart slow cooker with cooking spray. Place chicken in slow cooker. Cover and keep warm on low heat setting.

You can prepare and bake these yummy drummettes up to 24 hours ahead. Cover with foil and refrigerate. Reheat them in the slow cooker.

1 Appetizer: Calories 60 (Calories from Fat 25); Total Fat 3g (Saturated Fat 1g); Cholesterol 10mg; Sodium 115mg; Total Carbohydrate 4g (Dietary Fiber 0g); Protein 4g

Baked Buffalo Wings

Prep Time: 30 min ■ Start to Finish: 1 hr 15 min ■ 12 Servings

Chicken

2 lb chicken drummettes
   (about 24)
2 tablespoons honey
2 tablespoons ketchup
2 tablespoons red pepper sauce
1 tablespoon Worcestershire sauce
Paprika

Blue Cheese Dipping Sauce

$1/3$ cup low-fat cottage cheese
$1/2$ teaspoon white wine vinegar
2 tablespoons milk
1 tablespoon crumbled blue cheese
$1/8$ teaspoon white pepper
1 clove garlic, finely chopped

Celery sticks, if desired

1 Heat oven to 350°F. Line jelly roll pan, $15^{1}/_{2} \times 10^{1}/_{2} \times 1$ inch, with aluminum foil. Remove skin from chicken.

2 Mix honey, ketchup, pepper sauce and Worcestershire sauce in plastic bag with zipper top. Add chicken. Seal bag and refrigerate at least 15 minutes but no longer than 24 hours, turning occasionally.

3 To dipping sauce, place cottage cheese, vinegar, milk, half of the blue cheese, the white pepper and garlic in blender or food processor. Cover and blend on low speed until smooth and creamy. Spoon into serving dish. Stir in remaining blue cheese. Cover and refrigerate until serving time.

4 Place chicken in pan; sprinkle with paprika. Bake about 30 minutes or until crisp and juice of chicken is no longer pink when centers of thickest pieces are cut. Serve with celery sticks and sauce.

1 Serving: Calories 95 (Calories from Fat 40); Total Fat 4g (Saturated Fat 2g); Cholesterol 30mg; Sodium 125mg; Total Carbohydrate 4g (Dietary Fiber 0g); Protein 11g

Spicy Thai Chicken Wings

Prep Time: 25 min ▪ Start to Finish: 2 hrs 15 min ▪ 40 Appetizers

20 chicken wings or drummettes (about 4 lb)
1/4 cup dry sherry or chicken broth
1/4 cup oyster sauce
1/4 cup honey
3 tablespoons chopped fresh cilantro
2 tablespoons chili sauce
2 tablespoons grated lime peel
4 medium green onions, chopped (1/4 cup)
3 cloves garlic, finely chopped

1 Cut each chicken wing at joints to make 3 pieces; discard tip. Cut off and discard excess skin.

2 Mix remaining ingredients in resealable heavy-duty plastic food-storage bag or large glass bowl. Add chicken to marinade. Seal bag; turn to coat. Refrigerate at least 1 hour but no longer than 24 hours, turning once.

3 Heat oven to 375°F. Place chicken in ungreased jelly roll pan, 15 1/2×10 1/2×1 inch. Bake uncovered 30 minutes, stirring frequently. Bake about 20 minutes longer or until juice of chicken is no longer pink when centers of thickest pieces are cut.

1 Appetizer: Calories 60 (Calories from Fat 25); Total Fat 3g (Saturated Fat 1g); Cholesterol 15mg; Sodium 50mg; Total Carbohydrate 2g (Dietary Fiber 0g); Protein 5g

If you don't have oyster sauce,
you can use 2 tablespoons of soy sauce
instead; you can also use chicken broth
instead of the sherry.

Grilled Seasoned Chicken Drummettes

Prep Time: 10 min ▪ Start to Finish: 35 min ▪ 20 to 24 Appetizers

Chicken

1 container (16 oz) plain yogurt
1 tablespoon paprika
2 tablespoons curry powder
1 teaspoon garlic salt
20 to 24 chicken drummettes
  (about 2 lb)

Mint-Yogurt Dip

Remaining plain yogurt from
  16-oz container
¼ cup shredded peeled cucumber
1 clove garlic, finely chopped
½ teaspoon salt
½ teaspoon lemon juice
2 tablespoons chopped fresh
  mint leaves

1 Heat coals or gas grill for direct heat. Mix ½ cup of the yogurt, the paprika, curry powder and garlic salt in large bowl. Add chicken, stirring to coat all surfaces. Let stand 15 minutes.

2 To make dip, mix all ingredients in small bowl with spoon. Sprinkle with additional chopped fresh mint leaves if desired.

3 Cover and grill chicken 4 to 6 inches from medium heat 8 to 12 minutes, turning once or twice, until juice of chicken is no longer pink when centers of thickest pieces are cut. Serve with dip.

1 Appetizer: Calories 60 (Calories from Fat 25); Total Fat 2.5g (Saturated Fat 1g); Cholesterol 20mg; Sodium 125mg; Total Carbohydrate 2g (Dietary Fiber 0g); Protein 7g

Chipotle Chicken Drummettes

Prep Time: 15 min   Start to Finish: 1 hr 10 min   20 to 24 Appetizers

Chicken

1/4 cup chili sauce

2 tablespoons honey

1 tablespoon soy sauce

2 chipotle chiles in adobo sauce
    (from 7-oz can), chopped

2 teaspoons adobo sauce from can

1/4 teaspoon garlic powder

1/8 teaspoon coarsely ground pepper

2 lb chicken drummettes
    (20 to 24)

Avocado Mayonnaise

1 medium ripe avocado, peeled
    and pitted

2 tablespoons mayonnaise or
    salad dressing

1/4 cup chopped fresh cilantro

1 teaspoon lime juice

Dash of salt

1 Mix all ingredients except drummettes and Avocado Mayonnaise in shallow dish. Add drummettes; turn to coat. Cover and refrigerate 30 minutes to marinate.

2 Heat oven to 375°F. Line jelly roll pan, 15 1/2×10 1/2×1 inch, with aluminum foil. Spray foil with cooking spray. Remove drummettes from marinade; place in pan. Brush with remaining marinade. Bake 30 to 35 minutes or until chicken is no longer pink when centers of thickest pieces are cut.

3 Meanwhile, to make Avocado Mayonnaise, mash avocado in small bowl. Stir in remaining ingredients until well blended. Refrigerate until serving. Serve with warm drummettes.

1 Appetizer: Calories 85 (Calories from Fat 45); Total Fat 5g (Saturated Fat 1g); Cholesterol 20mg; Sodium 135mg; Total Carbohydrate 4g (Dietary Fiber 1g); Protein 6g

Maple Chicken Drummettes

Prep Time: 15 min ▪ Start to Finish: 1 hr 10 min ▪ 20 Appetizers

1/4 cup real maple syrup or honey
1/4 cup chili sauce
2 tablespoons chopped fresh chives
1 tablespoon soy sauce
1/2 teaspoon ground mustard
1/4 teaspoon ground red pepper (cayenne), if desired
2 lb chicken drummettes (about 20)

1 Heat oven to 375°F. Mix all ingredients except chicken. Place chicken in ungreased jelly roll pan, 15 1/2×10 1/2×1 inch. Pour syrup mixture over chicken; turn chicken to coat.

2 Bake uncovered 45 to 55 minutes, turning once and brushing with sauce after 30 minutes, until juice of chicken is no longer pink when centers of thickest pieces are cut. Serve chicken with sauce.

1 Appetizer: Calories 60 (Calories from Fat 20); Total Fat 2g (Saturated Fat 1g); Cholesterol 20mg; Sodium 100mg; Total Carbohydrate 4g (Dietary Fiber 0g); Protein 6g

For extra flavor, you can marinate the drummettes in the maple syrup mixture in a zippered plastic bag in the refrigerator for up to 1 hour. Then, just bake as directed.

Quick Chicken Quesadillas

Prep Time: 25 min ▪ Start to Finish: 25 min ▪ 4 Servings

1 package (6 oz) refrigerated cooked Southwest-flavor chicken breast strips
1/2 cup chunky-style salsa
8 flour tortillas (6 to 8 inch)
Cooking spray
2 cups finely shredded Colby–Monterey Jack cheese blend (8 oz)
1/4 cup sour cream

1 Cut chicken into bite-size pieces. In small bowl, mix chicken and salsa.

2 Spray 1 side of 1 tortilla with cooking spray; place sprayed side down in 10-inch skillet. Layer with 1/4 of the chicken mixture and 1/2 cup of the cheese. Top with another tortilla; spray top of tortilla with cooking spray.

3 Cook uncovered over medium heat 4 to 6 minutes, carefully turning after 2 minutes, until golden brown. Repeat with remaining tortillas, chicken mixture and cheese. To serve, cut quesadillas into wedges. Serve with sour cream and, if desired, additional salsa.

1 Serving: Calories 480 (Calories from Fat 250); Total Fat 28g (Saturated Fat 15g); Cholesterol 95mg; Sodium 920mg; Total Carbohydrate 30g (Dietary Fiber 2g); Protein 28g

Barbecue Pork Bites

Prep Time: 35 min ▪ Start to Finish: 50 min ▪ 8 Servings (4 pork pieces)

1 pork tenderloin (³/₄ to 1 lb)
1 tablespoon chili powder
1 teaspoon ground cumin
1 teaspoon packed brown sugar
¹/₄ teaspoon garlic powder
¹/₈ teaspoon ground red pepper (cayenne)
¹/₂ cup mayonnaise or salad dressing
¹/₂ teaspoon ground mustard
1 medium green onion, finely chopped (1 tablespoon)

1 Cut pork into 32 (1-inch) pieces; place in medium bowl. In small bowl, mix chili powder, cumin, brown sugar, garlic powder and red pepper. Reserve 2 teaspoons spice mixture; sprinkle remaining mixture over pork pieces; stir to coat completely. Let stand 15 minutes.

2 In small bowl, mix mayonnaise, mustard, reserved 2 teaspoons spice mixture and the onion; set aside.

3 Heat gas or charcoal grill. Spray grill basket (grill "wok") with cooking spray. Spoon pork into basket.

4 Place basket on grill. Cover grill; cook over medium heat 10 to 12 minutes, shaking basket or stirring pork once or twice, until pork is no longer pink in center. Serve with toothpicks and mayonnaise mixture for dipping.

To broil pork, set oven control to broil. Spray rack of broiler pan with cooking spray. Place pork on rack. Broil with tops 6 inches from heat about 10 minutes, turning once, until no longer pink in center.

1 Serving: Calories 160 (Calories from Fat 110); Total Fat 13g (Saturated Fat 2g); Cholesterol 30mg; Sodium 105mg; Total Carbohydrate 2g (Dietary Fiber 0g); Protein 10g

Mini Corn Dogs on a Stick

Prep Time: 30 min ▪ Start to Finish: 45 min ▪ 40 Servings (1 corn dog each)

40 wooden toothpicks
1 package (16 oz) cocktail-size hot dogs (about 40 pieces)
1 can (12 oz) refrigerated flaky biscuits (10 biscuits)
1 egg, beaten
1 tablespoon milk
1/2 cup cornmeal
1 tablespoon sugar
3/4 cup ketchup
3/4 cup yellow mustard

1 Heat oven to 400°F. Grease cookie sheet with shortening or spray with cooking spray. Insert toothpick into narrow end of each wiener. Separate dough into 10 biscuits; carefully divide each biscuit horizontally into 4 rounds. Wrap sides and top of each wiener with dough round, pinching edges to seal.

2 In pie plate, mix egg and milk. On a plate, mix cornmeal and sugar. Roll each wrapped wiener in egg mixture, then roll lightly in cornmeal mixture. Place seam side down on cookie sheet.

3 Bake 10 to 12 minutes or until tops are light golden brown and bottoms are golden brown. Remove from cookie sheet with spatula. Serve with ketchup and mustard.

1 Serving: Calories 80 (Calories from Fat 40); Total Fat 4.5g (Saturated Fat 1.5g); Cholesterol 10mg; Sodium 310mg; Total Carbohydrate 7g (Dietary Fiber 0g); Protein 2g

Southwest Riblets

Prep Time: 15 min ▪ Start to Finish: 1 hr 50 min ▪ About 42 Appetizers

2 tablespoons vegetable oil

1 small onion, chopped ($\frac{1}{4}$ cup)

$\frac{1}{2}$ teaspoon ground red pepper (cayenne)

2 cloves garlic, finely chopped

$\frac{1}{2}$ teaspoon salt

$\frac{1}{2}$ oz unsweetened baking chocolate, grated

1 cup water

2 tablespoons cider vinegar

1 can (6 oz) tomato paste

2 tablespoons sugar

3-lb rack fresh pork back ribs, cut lengthwise across bones in half

1 Heat oil in 1-quart saucepan over medium heat. Cook onion in oil 2 minutes, stirring frequently. Stir in red pepper, garlic and salt; reduce heat to low. Cover and cook 5 minutes, stirring occasionally. Stir in chocolate until melted.

2 Pour water, vinegar and tomato paste into food processor or blender. Add onion mixture and sugar. Cover and process, or blend, until well blended.

3 Heat oven to 375°F. Cut between pork back ribs to separate. Place in single layer in roasting pan. Pour sauce evenly over pork. Bake uncovered 30 minutes; turn pork. Bake 45 to 55 minutes longer or until ribs are tender.

1 Appetizer: Calories 80 (Calories from Fat 55); Total Fat 6g (Saturated Fat 2g); Cholesterol 20mg; Sodium 75mg; Total Carbohydrate 2g (Dietary Fiber 0g); Protein 5g

Grilled Veggies and Steak

Prep Time: 20 min ▪ Start to Finish: 30 min ▪ 4 Servings

1 package (6 oz) small fresh portabella mushrooms
$^1/_2$ lb beef sirloin steak (about $^3/_4$ inch thick), cut into $^3/_4$-inch cubes
1 cup frozen pearl onions (from 1-lb bag), thawed
$^1/_2$ cup plus 2 tablespoons balsamic vinaigrette
$^1/_2$ cup halved grape or cherry tomatoes

1 Heat gas or charcoal grill. In large bowl, place mushrooms, beef, onions and $^1/_2$ cup of the vinaigrette; toss to coat. Let stand 10 minutes; drain. Place mixture in grill basket (grill "wok"). Place basket on cookie sheet to carry to grill to catch drips.

2 Place basket on grill. Cover grill; cook over medium-high heat 7 to 9 minutes, shaking basket or stirring beef mixture twice, until vegetables are tender and beef is desired doneness. Stir in tomatoes.

3 Spoon beef mixture into serving dish. Stir in remaining 2 tablespoons vinaigrette.

1 Serving: Calories 150 (Calories from Fat 45); Total Fat 5g (Saturated Fat 1g); Cholesterol 30mg; Sodium 350mg; Total Carbohydrate 10g (Dietary Fiber 1g); Protein 15g

Appetizer Meatballs

Prep Time: 20 min ▪ Start to Finish: 40 min ▪ About 5 dozen meatballs

1 lb lean ground beef
1/2 lb ground pork
1 medium onion, finely chopped (1/2 cup)
1/4 cup plain bread crumbs
1/2 teaspoon ground mustard
1/2 teaspoon seasoned salt
1/8 teaspoon pepper
1 egg

1 Heat oven to 375°F. Spray jelly roll pan, 15 1/2×10 1/2×1 inch, with cooking spray. Mix all ingredients in large bowl. Shape into 1-inch meatballs. Place in pan.

2 Bake 15 to 20 minutes or until no longer pink in center and juice is clear. Cool completely. Cover tightly and refrigerate until ready to use. Use in sauce as desired.

Use those math skills—to easily divide the meat mixture, press it into 10×6-inch rectangle, then cut into 10 rows by 6 rows and shape into meatballs.

1 Meatball: Calories 30 (Calories from Fat 20); Total Fat 2g (Saturated Fat 1g); Cholesterol 10mg; Sodium 20mg; Total Carbohydrate 1g (Dietary Fiber 0g); Protein 2g

Baby Burgers

Prep Time: 30 min ▪ Start to Finish: 30 min ▪ 16 Appetizer burgers

1 lb lean (at least 80%) ground beef
2 teaspoons dried minced onion
1 teaspoon parsley flakes
3/4 teaspoon seasoned salt
4 slices (1 oz each) American cheese, cut into quarters
8 slices white bread, toasted, crusts trimmed, cut into quarters
16 thin slices plum (Roma) tomatoes (2 small), if desired
16 thin hamburger-style dill pickle slices, if desired
Ketchup, if desired
Mustard, if desired

1 Heat gas or charcoal grill. In medium bowl, mix beef, onion, parsley and seasoned salt. Divide into 16 portions. Shape each portion into a ball and flatten to 1/2-inch-thick patty, about 1 1/2 inches in diameter. On each of 4 (12-inch) metal skewers, thread 4 patties horizontally, leaving space between each.

2 Place patties on grill. Cover grill; cook over medium heat 8 to 10 minutes, turning once, until patties are no longer pink in center (160°F).

3 Top each burger with cheese piece. Place each burger on toast square. Top with tomato slice and another toast square. Place pickle slice on top; spear with toothpick to hold layers together. Serve with ketchup and mustard for dipping.

These cute little burgers can be mixed and shaped ahead of time. Just cover and refrigerate them until you are ready to grill. To broil patties, set oven control to broil. Thread patties on skewers as directed. Place patties on rack in broiler pan. Broil with tops 6 inches from heat 8 to 10 minutes, turning once, until no longer pink in center.

1 Burger: Calories 110 (Calories from Fat 50); Total Fat 6g (Saturated Fat 2.5g); Cholesterol 25mg; Sodium 270mg; Total Carbohydrate 7g (Dietary Fiber 0g); Protein 8g

keep it cool

4

Marinated Jicama Appetizer

Prep Time: 15 min ▪ Start to Finish: 2 hrs 15 min ▪ About 3¹/₂ dozen Appetizers

1 jicama (about 2 lb), peeled and cut into ³/₈-inch slices
¹/₄ cup lemon or lime juice
1 teaspoon salt
1 teaspoon chili powder

1 Cut jicama slices into desired shapes, using cookie cutters.

2 Arrange slices on serving plate. Drizzle with lemon juice. Sprinkle with salt and chili powder. Cover and refrigerate at least 2 hours to blend flavors.

Buy some time—you can cut the jicama shapes a day ahead. Toss them with lemon juice in a resealable plastic food-storage bag and refrigerate.

1 Appetizer: Calories 10 (Calories from Fat 0); Total Fat 0g (Saturated Fat 0g); Cholesterol 0mg; Sodium 60mg; Total Carbohydrate 3g (Dietary Fiber 1g); Protein 0g

Marinated Olives

Prep Time: 10 min ▪ Start to Finish: 48 hr 10 min ▪ 12 Servings

1 lb kalamata or other Greek olives
$1/4$ cup olive or vegetable oil
2 tablespoons chopped fresh parsley
2 tablespoons chopped fresh cilantro
1 tablespoon lemon juice
$1/2$ teaspoon crushed red pepper
2 cloves garlic, finely chopped

1 Rinse olives with cold water; drain. Place olives in 1-quart jar with tight-fitting lid. Mix remaining ingredients; pour over olives.

2 Cover tightly and refrigerate at least 48 hours but no longer than 2 weeks, turning jar upside down occasionally. Serve at room temperature.

1 Serving: Calories 10 (Calories from Fat 10); Total Fat 1g (Saturated Fat 0g); Cholesterol 0mg; Sodium 45mg; Total Carbohydrate 0g (Dietary Fiber 0g); Protein 0g

Mozzarella-Pepperoncini Platter

Prep Time: 15 min ▪ Start to Finish: 15 min ▪ 16 Servings

1 lb fresh reduced-fat mozzarella cheese, cut into $1/4$-inch slices

$2/3$ cup coarsely chopped drained garlic-dill Italian pepperoncini peppers (from 16-oz jar)

$1/3$ cup chopped drained roasted red bell peppers (from 7-oz jar)

16 thin slices French bread, lightly toasted, or whole-grain crackers

1 On serving platter, arrange mozzarella slices in a single layer.

2 Sprinkle pepperoncini peppers and bell peppers over cheese. Serve with bread.

If you prefer, you can also use regular mozzarella—whatever works for you.

1 Serving: Calories 110 (Calories from Fat 50); Total Fat 6g (Saturated Fat 3.5g); Cholesterol 15mg; Sodium 200mg; Total Carbohydrate 6g (Dietary Fiber 0g); Protein 8g

Antipasto Platter

Prep Time: 30 min ▪ Start to Finish: 30 min ▪ 24 Appetizers

12 slices hard-crusted round Italian bread or 24 slices French bread ($^{1}/_{2}$ inch thick)
2 cloves garlic
12 slices prosciutto or thinly sliced fully cooked ham (about 6 oz), cut in half
12 slices provolone cheese (about $^{3}/_{4}$ lb), cut in half
24 thin slices Genoa salami (about $^{3}/_{4}$ lb)
24 marinated mushrooms
24 marinated artichoke hearts
24 kalamata olives, pitted
$^{1}/_{3}$ cup olive or vegetable oil
$^{1}/_{2}$ medium lemon
1 tablespoon chopped fresh or $^{1}/_{2}$ teaspoon dried oregano leaves

1 If using Italian bread, cut each slice in half. Cut each garlic clove in half; rub cut sides over both sides of bread. Arrange bread and remaining ingredients except oil, lemon and oregano on serving platter.

2 To serve, top each bread slice with prosciutto, cheese, salami, mushroom, artichoke heart and olive. Drizzle with oil. Squeeze juice from lemon over top. Sprinkle with oregano.

1 Appetizer: Calories 200 (Calories from Fat 135); Total Fat 15g (Saturated Fat 5g); Cholesterol 25mg; Sodium 740mg; Total Carbohydrate 7g (Dietary Fiber 2g); Protein 10g

The gang will think they are in a restaurant! Bring out the extra-virgin olive oil and buy imported kalamata or Gaeta olives.

Three-Cheese Logs

Prep Time: 15 min ▪ Start to Finish: 2 hrs 15 min ▪ 20 Servings

1 package (8 oz) cream cheese, softened
1 tablespoon Worcestershire sauce
1 teaspoon ground mustard
2 cups shredded sharp Cheddar cheese (8 oz)
1/2 cup crumbled Stilton cheese
1/2 cup chopped drained roasted red bell peppers (from 7-oz jar)
1/4 cup chopped fresh chives
1/2 cup finely chopped walnuts or pecans
1 large apple, sliced
Assorted crackers

1 In large bowl, stir cream cheese, Worcestershire sauce and mustard until blended. Stir in Cheddar and Stilton cheeses, bell peppers and chives.

2 Divide cheese mixture in half. Shape each half into a log. Roll logs in walnuts. Wrap each log separately in plastic wrap or waxed paper. Refrigerate about 2 hours or until firm.

3 Place cheese logs on serving platter. Serve with apple slices and crackers.

1 Serving: Calories 150 (Calories from Fat 110); Total Fat 12g (Saturated Fat 6g); Cholesterol 25mg; Sodium 190mg; Total Carbohydrate 5g (Dietary Fiber 0g); Protein 5g

Amaretto Cheese-Filled Apricots

Prep Time: 20 min ▪ Start to Finish: 1 hr 20 min ▪ 30 Apricots

4 oz cream cheese (half of 8-oz package), softened
$1/3$ cup slivered almonds, toasted, chopped*
$1/4$ cup chopped dried cherries or sweetened dried cranberries
2 tablespoons amaretto liqueur or 1 teaspoon almond extract
      plus 2 tablespoons water
30 soft whole dried apricots

1 In small bowl, mix cream cheese, $1/4$ cup of the almonds, the cherries and amaretto with spoon. Spoon into small resealable food-storage plastic bag. Cut $1/2$ inch off 1 corner of bag.

2 With fingers, open apricots along one side so they resemble partially open clamshells. Pipe about 1 teaspoon cheese mixture into each apricot.

3 Finely chop remaining almonds. Dip cheese edge of apricots into almonds. Refrigerate 1 hour before serving to chill.

*To toast nuts, bake uncovered in ungreased shallow pan in 350°F oven 6 to 10 minutes, stirring occasionally, until light brown.

These filled apricots make a great addition to a cheese and fruit platter.

1 Apricot: Calories 45 (Calories from Fat 20); Total Fat 2g (Saturated Fat 1g); Cholesterol 0mg; Sodium 10mg; Total Carbohydrate 6g (Dietary Fiber 0g); Protein 0g

Chipotle Deviled Eggs

Prep Time: 20 min ▪ Start to Finish: 20 min ▪ 16 Appetizers

8 hard-cooked eggs
$1/4$ cup mayonnaise or salad dressing
$1/2$ teaspoon lemon juice
2 medium green onions, chopped (2 tablespoons)
2 teaspoons to 1 tablespoon finely chopped chipotle chiles in adobo sauce
    (from 7-oz can), drained
$1/8$ teaspoon salt
Paprika

1 Peel eggs; cut lengthwise in half. Slip out yolks and mash with fork.

2 Stir mayonnaise, lemon juice, onions, chiles and salt into yolks. Fill egg whites with egg yolk mixture, heaping it lightly. Sprinkle with paprika.

These little devils are spicy! You may want to warn your friends.

1 Appetizer: Calories 60 (Calories from Fat 45); Total Fat 5g (Saturated Fat 1g); Cholesterol 110mg; Sodium 75mg; Total Carbohydrate 1g (Dietary Fiber 0g); Protein 3g

Cucumber Slices Provençal

Prep Time: 10 min ▪ Start to Finish: 10 min ▪ 32 Appetizers

1 large English or burpless cucumber, chilled
1/3 cup sun-dried tomato spread
3 tablespoons crumbled chèvre (goat) cheese
32 small basil leaves

1 Make lines or indentations lengthwise down cucumber at 1/4-inch intervals, using vegetable peeler or tines of fork. Cut cucumber into 32 slices, 1/2 inch each. Place on paper towels to drain.

2 Spread each slice with about 1 teaspoon tomato spread. Sprinkle each with about 1/2 teaspoon cheese. Serve immediately, or refrigerate up to 1 hour. Top each slice with basil leaf just before serving.

It's worth it to buy the unwaxed, hydroponically grown English cucumbers because they have a sweet, delicate flavor and few or no seeds, but you can also use 2 medium cucumbers.

1 Appetizer: Calories 13 (Calories from Fat 10); Total Fat 1g (Saturated Fat 0g); Cholesterol 0mg; Sodium 25mg; Total Carbohydrate 1g (Dietary Fiber 0g); Protein 0g

Party Potatoes

Prep Time: 15 min ▪ Start to Finish: 1 hr 50 min ▪ 24 Servings

12 small new potatoes (about 1½ lb)
½ cup sour cream
Dill weed sprigs or chopped fresh chives

1 In 3-quart saucepan, heat 1 inch water to boiling. Add potatoes. Cover; heat to boiling. Reduce heat. Simmer 20 to 25 minutes or until tender; drain. Cool 30 minutes to 1 hour.

2 Cut potatoes in half; place cut sides up on serving tray. (Cut thin slice from bottom of each potato half, if necessary, to help stand upright.) Top each potato half with 1 teaspoon sour cream and dill weed sprig. Cover; refrigerate until serving.

1 Serving: Calories 30 (Calories from Fat 10); Total Fat 1g (Saturated Fat 0.5g); Cholesterol 0mg; Sodium 0mg; Total Carbohydrate 5g (Dietary Fiber 0g); Protein 0g

Greek Salad Pinwheels

Prep Time: 25 min ▪ Start to Finish: 2 hrs 25 min ▪ 48 Pinwheels

1 container (8 oz) garlic-and-herb whipped cream cheese
1 container (4 oz) crumbled feta cheese
$1/3$ cup finely chopped cucumber
6 flour tortillas for burritos, 8 inch (from 11.5-oz package)
$1/3$ cup pitted kalamata olives, coarsely chopped
3 small plum (Roma) tomatoes, chopped (about $1\frac{1}{2}$ cups)
3 cups fresh baby spinach leaves

1 In small bowl, beat cream cheese and feta cheese with electric mixer on medium speed until smooth. Stir in cucumber.

2 Place tortillas on microwavable plate or microwavable paper towel; microwave uncovered on High 10 to 15 seconds to soften. Spread about $1/4$ cup cheese mixture over each tortilla. Top evenly with olives and tomatoes. Arrange $1/2$ cup spinach on each tortilla to within $1/2$ inch of edge. Roll up tightly; wrap in plastic wrap. Refrigerate 2 to 3 hours to blend flavors.

3 Trim ends of rolled tortillas if desired. Cut each roll into eight 1-inch slices. Arrange with cut sides down on serving dish.

1 Pinwheel: Calories 45 (Calories from Fat 25); Total Fat 2.5g (Saturated Fat 1.5g); Cholesterol 5mg; Sodium 85mg; Total Carbohydrate 4g (Dietary Fiber 0g); Protein 1g

Italian Chop Salad in Shells

Prep Time: 55 min ▪ Start to Finish: 55 min ▪ 36 Appetizers

1 package (16 oz) jumbo pasta shells
4 cups chopped romaine
1/2 cup chopped fresh basil leaves
1 cup coarsely chopped cooked chicken
1 large tomato, coarsely chopped (1 cup)
1 medium cucumber, coarsely chopped (3/4 cup)
1 package (3 oz) Italian salami, chopped
1/3 cup roasted garlic Italian vinaigrette

1 Cook pasta shells as directed on package; drain and cool.

2 Place remaining ingredients except vinaigrette in medium bowl. Pour vinaigrette over salad; toss to coat.

3 Stuff shells with salad. Cover and refrigerate up to 2 hours before serving.

Want a change? Try 3 ounces of pepperoni, chopped, instead of the Italian salami.

1 Appetizer: Calories 70 (Calories from Fat 20); Total Fat 2g (Saturated Fat 1g); Cholesterol 5mg; Sodium 65mg; Total Carbohydrate 11g (Dietary Fiber 1g); Protein 3g

Margarita Shrimp Cocktail

Prep Time: 25 min ▪ Start to Finish: 2 hrs 30 min ▪ About 26 Shrimp

Shrimp

1½ lb medium shrimp with shells
  (26 to 30 shrimp)
4 cups water
2 teaspoons salt
1½ cups dry white wine or
  nonalcoholic wine
2 tablespoons lime juice
5 black peppercorns
Handful of fresh cilantro

Sauce

½ cup orange juice
½ cup ketchup
¼ cup chopped fresh cilantro
¼ cup lime juice
¼ cup lemon juice
2 tablespoons tequila, if desired
2 tablespoons vegetable oil
½ teaspoon salt
⅛ teaspoon freshly ground pepper
Dash of red pepper sauce

1 Peel shrimp, leaving tails intact; reserve shells. Using a small, pointed knife or shrimp deveiner, make shallow cut lengthwise down back of each shrimp, then wash out the vein.

2 In 4-quart Dutch oven, heat shrimp shells, 4 cups water and 2 teaspoons salt to boiling over high heat. Add wine, 2 tablespoons lime juice, the peppercorns and handful of cilantro. Reduce heat to medium. Cover and cook 30 minutes.

3 Strain stock into large bowl and discard shells, peppercorns and cilantro. Return stock to pot and heat to boiling over high heat. Add shrimp; remove pan from heat. Cover and let stand 8 to 10 minutes until shrimp are pink and firm.

4 Meanwhile, fill large bowl half full with ice and water. When shrimp are done, remove and plunge into ice bath to chill. (You can keep stock for another purpose.)

5 In medium nonreactive bowl, mix all sauce ingredients. Stir in cooked shrimp to coat. Cover and refrigerate at least 30 minutes but no longer than 3 hours. Serve cold.

1 Shrimp: Calories 30 (Calories from Fat 10); Total Fat 1g (Saturated Fat 0g); Cholesterol 25mg; Sodium 170mg; Total Carbohydrate 2g (Dietary Fiber 0g); Protein 3g

Cucumber, Carrot and Smoked Salmon Crudités

Prep Time: 20 min   Start to Finish: 20 min   24 Appetizers

2 oz salmon lox, finely chopped
$^1/_2$ package (8-oz size) cream cheese, softened
$^3/_4$ teaspoon chopped fresh or $^1/_4$ teaspoon dried dill weed
1 large cucumber, cut into $^1/_4$-inch slices (12 slices)
1 large carrot, cut into $^1/_4$-inch slices (12 slices)
Crackers, if desired
Dill weed sprigs, if desired

1 Mix lox, cream cheese and chopped dill weed.

2 Place lox mixture in decorating bag fitted with large star tip; pipe heaping teaspoonful onto each cucumber and carrot slice or cracker. (Or spoon on cream cheese mixture.) Garnish each with dill weed sprig.

Go totally fancy—cut the cucumber slices with a small star-shaped cookie cutter and use a decorating bag. Or not—just mound the mix on a simple slice.

1 Appetizer: Calories 25 (Calories from Fat 20); Total Fat 2g (Saturated Fat 1g); Cholesterol 5mg; Sodium 35mg; Total Carbohydrate 2g (Dietary Fiber 0g); Protein 1g

Dilled Salmon

Prep Time: 25 min ▪ Start to Finish: 1 hr 45 min ▪ 16 Servings

Salmon

2 lb fresh salmon, skin removed
1 teaspoon dried dill weed
1/2 teaspoon salt
1/4 teaspoon onion powder
1/4 teaspoon garlic powder
1/4 teaspoon pepper
3/4 cup water

Dill Sauce

1 1/2 cups sour cream
3/4 cup chopped seeded cucumber
4 medium green onions, chopped
    (1/4 cup)
1 tablespoon dried dill weed
1/4 teaspoon salt
1/2 teaspoon grated lemon peel
1/2 teaspoon lemon juice

1 Rinse salmon; pat dry. Place salmon in 12-inch skillet. In small bowl, mix 1 teaspoon dill weed, 1/2 teaspoon salt, the onion powder, garlic powder and pepper; sprinkle over salmon. Carefully pour water around salmon until 1/4 to 1/2 inch deep.

2 Cover and cook salmon over medium heat 10 to 12 minutes or until salmon flakes easily with fork; carefully drain.

3 Remove salmon from skillet with 2 large slotted spatulas; place on serving plate. Use paper towels to remove any excess cooking liquid from salmon and plate. Refrigerate about 1 hour or until chilled.

4 Meanwhile, in medium bowl, mix all sauce ingredients. Cover and refrigerate until serving. Serve sauce with salmon.

1 Serving: Calories 110 (Calories from Fat 60); Total Fat 7g (Saturated Fat 3.5g); Cholesterol 45mg; Sodium 150mg; Total Carbohydrate 1g (Dietary Fiber 0g); Protein 11g

Chicken Salad Roll-Ups

Prep Time: 35 min ▪ Start to Finish: 1 hr 35 min ▪ 24 Appetizers

2 cups chopped cooked chicken
3 medium green onions, chopped (3 tablespoons)
1/4 cup chopped walnuts
1/2 cup creamy poppy seed dressing
1/2 cup cream cheese spread (from 8-oz container)
2 flour tortillas (9 or 10 inch)
6 leaves Bibb lettuce
1/2 cup finely chopped strawberries

1 Mix chicken, onions and walnuts in food processor bowl. Cover and process by using quick on-and-off motions until finely chopped. Add 1/3 cup of the poppy seed dressing; process only until mixed. Mix remaining dressing and the cream cheese spread in small bowl with spoon until smooth.

2 Spread cream cheese mixture evenly over entire surface of tortillas. Remove white rib from lettuce leaves. Press lettuce into cream cheese, tearing to fit and leaving top 2 inches of tortillas uncovered. Spread chicken mixture over lettuce. Sprinkle strawberries over chicken.

3 Firmly roll up tortillas, beginning at bottom. Wrap each roll in plastic wrap. Refrigerate at least 1 hour. Trim ends of each roll. Cut rolls into 1/2- to 3/4-inch slices.

1 Appetizer: Calories 70 (Calories from Fat 35); Total Fat 4g (Saturated Fat 1.5g); Cholesterol 20mg; Sodium 50mg; Total Carbohydrate 5g (Dietary Fiber 0g); Protein 4g

Prosciutto-Pesto Napoleons

Prep Time: 25 min ▪ Start to Finish: 1 hr 25 min ▪ 24 Napoleons

1 sheet frozen puff pastry (from 17.3-oz box)

1 egg, beaten

1 tablespoon sesame seed

¼ cup refrigerated basil pesto (from 7-oz container)

1 cup roasted red bell peppers (from 7-oz jar), drained, cut into thin strips and
    drained on paper towels

¼ lb thinly sliced prosciutto, cut crosswise into strips

1 Thaw pastry at room temperature 30 minutes. Heat oven to 400°F.
Unfold pastry; brush top with beaten egg. Sprinkle with sesame seed.
Cut pastry into thirds along fold lines. Cut each strip crosswise into
8 rectangles, each 3×1¼ inches. On ungreased cookie sheets, place rectangles
2 inches apart.

2 Bake about 15 minutes or until puffed and golden brown. Remove from
cookie sheets to wire rack. Cool completely, about 15 minutes.

3 Cut each rectangle in half horizontally. Spread ½ teaspoon pesto on cut
side of bottom of each rectangle. Top with bell peppers and prosciutto
strips. Place tops of rectangles over prosciutto.

1 Napoleon: Calories 80 (Calories from Fat 50); Total Fat 5g (Saturated Fat 1.5g); Cholesterol 20mg;
Sodium 105mg; Total Carbohydrate 5g (Dietary Fiber 0g); Protein 2g

Roast Beef Bruschetta

Prep Time: 20 min ▪ Start to Finish: 30 min ▪ 6 Servings (5 bruschetta each)

1 loaf (1 lb) baguette French bread, cut into 30 ($\frac{1}{4}$-inch) slices
2 tablespoons olive or vegetable oil
$\frac{1}{2}$ cup chive-and-onion cream cheese spread (from 8-oz container)
$\frac{1}{2}$ lb thinly sliced cooked roast beef
$\frac{1}{4}$ teaspoon coarsely ground pepper
4 plum (Roma) tomatoes, thinly sliced
8 medium green onions, sliced ($\frac{1}{2}$ cup)

1 Heat oven to 375°F. Brush both sides of bread slices with oil. Place on ungreased cookie sheet. Bake about 5 minutes or until crisp. Cool 5 minutes.

2 Spread cream cheese over each bread slice. Top with beef; sprinkle with pepper. Top with tomato slice and onions.

Get a running start—toast the bread slices a day ahead, and store loosely covered at room temperature. Top them up to 1 hour ahead, then cover and place in the fridge until serving.

1 Serving: Calories 400 (Calories from Fat 170); Total Fat 19g (Saturated Fat 7g); Cholesterol 45mg; Sodium 600mg; Total Carbohydrate 41g (Dietary Fiber 3g); Protein 18g

Beef and Spinach Roll-Ups

Prep Time: 15 min ▪ Start to Finish: 15 min ▪ 24 Appetizers

¹/₄ cup mayonnaise or salad dressing
¹/₂ teaspoon garlic powder
2 spinach-flavored tortillas (9 or 10 inch)
1 cup fresh spinach
¹/₄ lb thinly sliced cooked roast beef
³/₄ cup shredded Cheddar cheese (3 oz)
1 medium tomato, chopped

1 Mix mayonnaise and garlic powder in small bowl. Spread mixture evenly over tortillas.

2 Top tortillas with layers of spinach, beef, cheese and tomato; roll up tightly. Trim ends from rolls. Cut each roll into 12 slices; secure with toothpicks. Serve immediately or refrigerate until serving.

You can use plain flour tortillas instead of the spinach-flavored ones if you like.

1 Appetizer: Calories 65 (Calories from Fat 45); Total Fat 5g (Saturated Fat 2g); Cholesterol 10mg; Sodium 65mg; Total Carbohydrate 2g (Dietary Fiber 0g); Protein 3g

Fruit Kabobs with Tropical Fruit Coulis

Marinated Havarti Cheese Kabobs

Vegetable Kabobs with Mustard Dip

Surf and Turf Kabobs

Italian Tortellini Kabobs

Vegetable Pot Stickers

Cheesy Potato Skins

Sweet Potato Mini-Latkes

Brie and Cherry Pastry Cups

Gorgonzola- and Hazelnut-Stuffed Mushrooms

Black Bean and Corn Wonton Cups

Chewy Pizza Bread

Filled Rice Fritters

Mini Pork Tacos

Empanadillas

Spiced Pork Tenderloin Crostini

Spicy Lemon Shrimp with Basil Mayonnaise

5

skewers and finger foods

Fruit Kabobs with Tropical Fruit Coulis

Prep Time: 40 min ▪ Start to Finish: 40 min ▪ 24 Kabobs

6 cups bite-size pieces assorted fresh fruit (pineapple, watermelon and
    cantaloupe)
1 cup green grapes
1 cup blueberries
3 small starfruit, cut into 24 slices
2 large mangoes, peeled, seeds removed and cut into pieces
1/4 cup pineapple preserves

1 Thread 4 to 6 pieces of fruits (except mangoes) on each of twenty-four 6-inch skewers. Place skewers on large serving platter; set aside.

2 Place mango pieces and pineapple preserves in food processor. Cover and process until smooth; pour into small serving bowl. Serve kabobs with mango coulis.

Be mellow—instead of making the kabobs, serve the fruit in a large glass bowl with the coulis in a separate bowl. Set out toothpicks, and nosh away.

1 Kabob: Calories 45 (Calories from Fat 0); Total Fat 0g (Saturated Fat 0g); Cholesterol 0mg; Sodium 5mg; Total Carbohydrate 11g (Dietary Fiber 1g); Protein 0g

Marinated Havarti Cheese Kabobs

Prep Time: 15 min ■ Start to Finish: 45 min ■ 16 Kabobs

4 slices (1/2 inch thick) English cucumber, cut crosswise in half
8 oz Havarti cheese, cut into 1/2- to 3/4-inch cubes (32 cubes)
1/2 cup balsamic vinaigrette
8 pitted Kalamata or ripe olives
16 red and/or yellow cherry tomatoes or yellow pear tomatoes

1 Mix cucumber, cheese and vinaigrette in shallow dish. Let stand at room temperature 30 minutes to marinate.

2 Thread 1 cucumber piece or olive, 2 cheese cubes and 1 tomato on each of 16 small cocktail skewers. Serve immediately, or refrigerate until ready to serve.

You can use any firm cheese to substitute for the Havarti—try Gouda, Cheddar, Colby or mozzarella.

1 Kabob: Calories 90 (Calories from Fat 70); Total Fat 8g (Saturated Fat 4g); Cholesterol 15mg; Sodium 170mg; Total Carbohydrate 2g (Dietary Fiber 0g); Protein 3g

Vegetable Kabobs with Mustard Dip

Prep Time: 35 min ▪ Start to Finish: 1 hr 35 min ▪ 9 Servings

Dip

¹⁄₂ cup sour cream

¹⁄₂ cup plain yogurt

1 tablespoon finely chopped
    fresh parsley

1 teaspoon onion powder

1 teaspoon garlic salt

1 tablespoon Dijon mustard

Kabobs

1 medium bell pepper, cut into
    6 strips, then cut into thirds
    (18 pieces)

1 medium zucchini, cut diagonally
    into ¹⁄₂-inch slices

8 oz fresh whole mushrooms

9 large cherry tomatoes

2 tablespoons olive or vegetable oil

1 In small bowl, mix all dip ingredients. Cover; refrigerate at least 1 hour.

2 Heat gas or charcoal grill. On 5 (12-inch) metal skewers, thread vegetables so that one kind of vegetable is on the same skewer (use 2 skewers for mushrooms); leave space between each piece. Brush vegetables with oil.

3 Place skewers of bell pepper and zucchini on grill. Cover grill; cook over medium heat 2 minutes. Add skewers of mushrooms and tomatoes. Cover grill; cook 4 to 5 minutes, carefully turning every 2 minutes, until vegetables are tender. Remove vegetables from skewers to serving plate. Serve with dip.

1 Serving: Calories 80 (Calories from Fat 50); Total Fat 6g (Saturated Fat 2g); Cholesterol 10mg; Sodium 170mg; Total Carbohydrate 5g (Dietary Fiber 1g); Protein 2g

Choose red bell peppers for beautiful color and a sweeter flavor than green bell pepper.

Surf and Turf Kabobs

Prep Time: 15 min ▪ Start to Finish: 50 min ▪ 12 Kabobs

$3/4$ lb beef boneless sirloin ($3/4$ inch thick), trimmed of fat
12 uncooked peeled deveined medium or large shrimp, thawed if frozen
    and tails removed
$1/2$ cup teriyaki marinade and sauce (from 10-oz bottle)
$1/4$ teaspoon coarsely ground pepper

1 Cut beef into 24 (1-inch) pieces. Mix beef, shrimp and teriyaki sauce in medium bowl. Sprinkle with pepper. Cover and refrigerate 30 minutes, stirring frequently, to marinate. Meanwhile, soak twelve 4- to 6-inch wooden skewers in water 30 minutes to prevent burning.

2 Spray broiler pan rack with cooking spray. Thread 1 beef piece, 1 shrimp and another beef piece on each skewer, reserving marinade. Place kabobs on rack in broiler pan.

3 Broil kabobs with tops 4 to 6 inches from heat 5 to 6 minutes, turning once and basting with marinade once or twice, until shrimp are pink and firm. Discard any remaining marinade.

For fun, you can also serve these meat and seafood kabobs with a variety of sauces. Try small bowls of teriyaki sauce, sweet-and-sour sauce and horseradish-mustard sauce.

1 Kabob: Calories 40 (Calories from Fat 10); Total Fat 1g (Saturated Fat 0g); Cholesterol 25mg; Sodium 330mg; Total Carbohydrate 1g (Dietary Fiber 0g); Protein 7g

Italian Tortellini Kabobs

Prep Time: 30 min ▪ Start to Finish: 30 min ▪ 12 Kabobs

12 uncooked refrigerated or dried cheese-filled tomato- or spinach-flavor tortellini
¼ cup drained roasted red bell peppers (from 7-oz jar)
¼ cup grated Parmesan cheese
3 tablespoons Italian dressing
4-oz piece salami, cut into twelve 1-inch wedges
2-oz piece mozzarella cheese, cut into twelve ¾-inch cubes
12 pieces marinated artichoke hearts (from two 6- to 7-oz jars), drained
12 cherry tomatoes

1 Cook and drain tortellini as directed on package; cool.

2 Place bell peppers in blender. Cover and blend until smooth. Add Parmesan cheese and Italian dressing. Cover and blend until smooth. Pour mixture into large plastic or glass bowl. Stir in tortellini, salami, mozzarella cheese, artichoke hearts and tomatoes.

3 Thread tortellini, mozzarella cheese, salami, artichoke hearts and tomatoes alternately on each of twelve 4- to 6-inch skewers. Serve immediately, or cover and refrigerate up to 24 hours.

It's a surprise kabob! Break out of the ordinary with these easy kabobs that you don't even have to grill.

1 Kabob: Calories 95 (Calories from Fat 55); Total Fat 6g (Saturated Fat 2g); Cholesterol 25mg; Sodium 240mg; Total Carbohydrate 6g (Dietary Fiber 1g); Protein 5g

Vegetable Pot Stickers

Prep Time: 55 min ▪ Start to Finish: 55 min ▪ 10 Servings (3 pot stickers each)

1 1/2 cups chicken broth
1 medium onion, finely chopped (1/2 cup)
1 medium stalk celery, finely chopped (1/2 cup)
1/2 cup thinly sliced cabbage
1/2 cup chopped mushrooms
1 teaspoon grated gingerroot
2 cloves garlic, finely chopped
1 teaspoon soy sauce
1 teaspoon dark sesame oil
1/2 package (16-oz size) wonton skins (30 skins)

1 Heat 3/4 cup of the broth to boiling in 10-inch nonstick skillet over medium-high heat. Stir in onion, celery, cabbage, mushrooms, gingerroot and garlic. Cook 5 to 8 minutes, stirring frequently and adding more broth if vegetables begin to stick, until vegetables are tender. Remove from heat. Stir in soy sauce and sesame oil. Remove vegetable mixture from skillet. Wash and dry skillet.

2 Brush edges of one wonton skin with water. Place 1 heaping teaspoon vegetable mixture on center of skin. Fold skin in half over filling and pinch edges to seal. Make creases in sealed edges to form pleats on one side of each pot sticker. Repeat with remaining wonton skins and vegetable mixture. (If making ahead, cover and refrigerate up to 24 hours.)

3 Spray skillet with cooking spray; heat skillet over medium heat. Cook pot stickers in skillet, pleated sides up, about 1 minute or until bottoms are light brown. Add remaining 3/4 cup broth. Cover and cook 5 to 8 minutes or until most of the liquid is absorbed.

Love making pot stickers and other dumplings?

You might want to buy a dumpling maker. These gadgets make quick work of filling, folding and crimping.

1 Serving: Calories 10 (Calories from Fat 0); Total Fat 0g (Saturated Fat 0g); Cholesterol 0mg; Sodium 70mg; Total Carbohydrate 3g (Dietary Fiber 0g); Protein 1g

Cheesy Potato Skins

Prep Time: 26 min ▮ Start to Finish: 1 hr 45 min ▮ 8 Servings

4 large potatoes (about 2 lb)
2 tablespoons butter or margarine, melted
1 cup shredded Colby–Monterey Jack cheese blend (4 oz)
$1/2$ cup sour cream
8 medium green onions, sliced ($1/2$ cup)

1 Heat oven to 375°F. Prick potatoes with fork. Bake potatoes 1 hour to 1 hour 15 minutes or until tender. Let stand until cool enough to handle.

2 Cut potatoes lengthwise into fourths; carefully scoop out pulp, leaving $1/4$-inch shells. Refrigerate potato pulp for another use.

3 Set oven control to broil. Place potato shells, skin sides down, on rack in broiler pan. Brush with butter.

4 Broil with tops 4 to 5 inches from heat 8 to 10 minutes or until crisp and brown. Sprinkle cheese over potato shells. Broil about 30 seconds longer or until cheese is melted. Serve hot with sour cream and green onions.

Buy pre-shredded cheese—it's a real time saver.

1 Serving: Calories 120 (Calories from Fat 45); Total Fat 5g (Saturated Fat 3g); Cholesterol 15mg; Sodium 90mg; Total Carbohydrate 13g (Dietary Fiber 1g); Protein 4g

Sweet Potato Mini-Latkes

Prep Time: 20 min   ▪   Start to Finish: 35 min   ▪   About 30 Appetizers

2 medium sweet potatoes (1 lb), peeled and shredded
2 medium green onions, finely chopped (2 tablespoons)
$\frac{1}{4}$ cup all-purpose flour
$\frac{1}{2}$ teaspoon salt
$\frac{1}{4}$ teaspoon pepper
1 egg, slightly beaten
1 cup sour cream
Sliced pecans, if desired

1 Heat oven to 400°F. Grease cookie sheet. Mix all ingredients except sour cream and pecans.

2 Drop sweet potato mixture by teaspoonfuls onto cookie sheet; flatten slightly. Bake 12 to 15 minutes, turning once, until golden brown. Top with sour cream. Garnish with pecans.

1 Appetizer: Calories 30 (Calories from Fat 10); Total Fat 1g (Saturated Fat 1g); Cholesterol 10mg; Sodium 45mg; Total Carbohydrate 4g (Dietary Fiber 0g); Protein 1g

Brie and Cherry Pastry Cups

Prep Time: 30 min ▪ Start to Finish: 55 min ▪ 36 Appetizers

1 sheet frozen puff pastry (from 17.3-oz package), thawed
1/3 to 1/2 cup red cherry preserves
4 oz Brie cheese, cut into 1/2 x 1/2-inch pieces (36 pieces)
1/4 cup chopped pecans
2 tablespoons chopped fresh chives

1 Heat oven to 375°F. Spray 36 miniature muffin cups, 1³/₄×1 inch, with cooking spray. Cut pastry into 36 (1¹/₂-inch) squares. Slightly press each square into muffin cup; press center with finger.

2 Bake 10 minutes. Press center with handle of wooden spoon. Bake 6 to 8 minutes longer or until golden brown. Immediately press again in center. Fill each with about ¹/₂ teaspoon preserves. Top with cheese piece, pecans and chives.

3 Bake 3 to 5 minutes or until cheese is melted. Serve warm.

If you like spicy foods, try substituting red or green jalapeño jelly for the cherry preserves. It's a sweet and spicy treat!

1 Appetizer: Calories 60 (Calories from Fat 35); Total Fat 4g (Saturated Fat 1g); Cholesterol 10mg; Sodium 35mg; Total Carbohydrate 5g (Dietary Fiber 0g); Protein 1g

Gorgonzola- and Hazelnut- Stuffed Mushrooms

Prep Time: 30 min ▪ Start to Finish: 50 min ▪ About 35 Mushrooms

1 lb fresh whole mushrooms
1/3 cup crumbled Gorgonzola cheese
1/4 cup Italian-style bread crumbs
1/4 cup chopped hazelnuts (filberts)
1/4 cup finely chopped red bell pepper
4 medium green onions, chopped (1/4 cup)
1/2 teaspoon salt

1 Heat oven to 350°F. Remove stems from mushroom caps; reserve caps. Finely chop enough stems to measure about 1/2 cup. Discard remaining stems.

2 Mix chopped mushroom stems and remaining ingredients in small bowl until well blended. Spoon into mushroom caps, mounding slightly. Place in ungreased jelly roll pan, 15 1/2×10 1/2×1 inch.

3 Bake 15 to 20 minutes or until thoroughly heated. Serve warm.

1 Mushroom: Calories 20 (Calories from Fat 10); Total Fat 1g (Saturated Fat 0g); Cholesterol 0mg; Sodium 60mg; Total Carbohydrate 1g (Dietary Fiber 0g); Protein 1g

Black Bean and Corn Wonton Cups

Prep Time: 25 min ▪ Start to Finish: 35 min ▪ 36 Appetizers

36 wonton skins
²/₃ cup chunky-style salsa
¹/₄ cup chopped fresh cilantro
¹/₂ teaspoon ground cumin
¹/₂ teaspoon chili powder
1 can (15¹/₄ oz) whole kernel corn, drained
1 can (15 oz) black beans, rinsed and drained
¹/₄ cup plus 2 tablespoons sour cream
Cilantro sprigs, if desired

1 Heat oven to 350°F. Gently fit 1 wonton skin into each of 36 small muffin cups, 1³/₄×1 inch, pressing against bottom and side. Bake 8 to 10 minutes or until light golden brown. Remove from pan; cool on wire rack.

2 Mix remaining ingredients except sour cream and cilantro sprigs. Just before serving, spoon bean mixture into wonton cups. Top each with ¹/₂ teaspoon sour cream. Garnish each with cilantro sprig.

1 Appetizer: Calories 55 (Calories from Fat 10); Total Fat 1g (Saturated Fat 0g); Cholesterol 5mg; Sodium 90mg; Total Carbohydrate 10g (Dietary Fiber 1g); Protein 2g

Chewy Pizza Bread

Prep Time: 10 min ▪ Start to Finish: 30 min ▪ 4 Servings (4 squares each)

1 1/2 cups all-purpose flour
1 1/2 teaspoons baking powder
1/2 teaspoon salt
3/4 cup regular or nonalcoholic beer
1/2 cup tomato pasta sauce
1/3 cup shredded mozzarella cheese (1.5 oz)
Chopped fresh basil leaves, if desired

1 Heat oven to 425°F. Spray 8-inch square pan with cooking spray.

2 In medium bowl, mix flour, baking powder and salt. Stir in beer just until flour is moistened. Spread dough in pan. Spread pasta sauce over dough. Sprinkle with cheese.

3 Bake 15 to 20 minutes or until toothpick inserted in center comes out clean. Sprinkle with basil. Cut into 2-inch squares. Serve warm.

1 Serving: Calories 230 (Calories from Fat 30); Total Fat 3.5g (Saturated Fat 1.5g); Cholesterol 5mg; Sodium 680mg; Total Carbohydrate 43g (Dietary Fiber 2g); Protein 8g

Filled Rice Fritters

Prep Time: 1 hr 20 min ▪ Start to Finish: 1 hr 20 min ▪ About 48 Fritters

5 cups chicken broth
2 cups uncooked Arborio rice
2 eggs, beaten
¼ cup freshly grated imported Parmesan cheese
1 tablespoon butter or margarine, softened
48 cubes (½ inch) mozzarella cheese
¼ cup ¼-inch cubes imported prosciutto or fully cooked ham (about 2 oz)
¼ cup ¼-inch cubes mushrooms
1 cup Italian-style dry bread crumbs
Vegetable oil

1 Heat broth and rice to boiling 3-quart saucepan; reduce heat. Cover and simmer about 20 minutes or until liquid is absorbed (do not lift cover or stir). Spread rice on ungreased cookie sheet; cool.

2 Mix rice, eggs, Parmesan cheese and butter. Shape into 1½-inch balls. Press 1 cube mozzarella cheese, 1 cube prosciutto and 1 cube mushroom in center of each ball; reshape to cover cubes completely. Roll balls in bread crumbs to coat.

3 Heat oil (2 inches) in deep fryer or Dutch oven to 375°F. Fry 5 or 6 fritters at a time about 2 minutes or until deep golden brown; drain on paper towels.

When you break into these stuffed rice fritters, the melted cheese inside pulls into threads that look like telephone cords. That's how they got the name in Rome of *suppli al telefono* — telephone cord.

1 Fritter: Calories 75 (Calories from Fat 25); Total Fat 3g (Saturated Fat 1g); Cholesterol 10mg; Sodium 160mg; Total Carbohydrate 9g (Dietary Fiber 0g); Protein 3g

Mini Pork Tacos

Prep Time: 20 min ▪ Start to Finish: 8 hr 20 min ▪ 24 Appetizers

2¹/₂-lb pork boneless loin roast
1 medium onion, thinly sliced
2 cups barbecue sauce
³/₄ cup salsa
3 tablespoons chili powder
1 tablespoon Mexican seasoning
1 package (3.8 oz) miniature taco shells (24 shells), heated
Assorted toppings (shredded Cheddar cheese, chopped green onions,
      chopped fresh cilantro, cooked black beans, sour cream)

1 Remove excess fat from pork. Place pork in 3¹/₂- to 6-quart slow cooker; top with onion. Mix remaining ingredients except taco shells and toppings; pour over pork.

2 Cover and cook on low heat setting 8 to 10 hours or until pork is very tender.

3 Remove pork; place on large plate. Use 2 forks to pull pork into shreds. Stir pork back into slow cooker. Spoon pork mixture into taco shells. Serve with toppings.

Relax—serve the shredded pork right in the slow cooker on the
      low heat setting, and let your guests make their own mini tacos.
      Set out a variety of your favorite Mexican toppings so folks can
      make their tacos exactly as they like.

1 Appetizer: Calories 150 (Calories from Fat 55); Total Fat 6g (Saturated Fat 2g); Cholesterol 35mg;
Sodium 320mg; Total Carbohydrate 13g (Dietary Fiber 1g); Protein 12g

Empanadillas

Prep Time: 40 min ▪ Start to Finish: 1 hr 5 min ▪ 24 Appetizers

8 oz bulk spicy pork sausage
1 medium onion, finely chopped ($1/2$ cup)
1 teaspoon finely chopped garlic
$1/4$ cup raisins, finely chopped
$1/4$ cup pitted green olives, finely chopped
1 teaspoon ground cumin
1 package (17.3 oz) frozen puff pastry, thawed
1 egg
1 teaspoon water
Fresh cilantro, if desired

1 Heat oven to 400°F. Line large cookie sheet with foil or cooking parchment paper; lightly spray with cooking spray.

2 In 10-inch skillet, cook sausage, onion and garlic over medium-high heat 5 to 7 minutes, stirring occasionally, until sausage is no longer pink. Stir in raisins, olives and cumin; remove from heat.

3 On lightly floured surface, roll 1 sheet of pastry into 12×9-inch rectangle, trimming edges if necessary. Cut into twelve 3-inch squares.

4 Place 1 tablespoon sausage mixture on each pastry square. In small bowl, beat egg and water with fork until well blended. Brush egg mixture on edges of pastry squares. Fold pastry over filling to make triangles; press edges with fork to seal. Place on cookie sheet. Repeat with remaining pastry and sausage mixture. Brush tops of triangles with egg mixture.

5 Bake 20 to 25 minutes or until golden brown. Serve warm. Garnish with cilantro.

1 Appetizer: Calories 140 (Calories from Fat 90); Total Fat 10g (Saturated Fat 3.5g); Cholesterol 35mg; Sodium 110mg; Total Carbohydrate 11g (Dietary Fiber 0g); Protein 3g

For a less spicy version, substitute ground beef or ground turkey for the sausage.

Spiced Pork Tenderloin Crostini

Prep Time: 30 min ▪ Start to Finish: 1 hr 10 min ▪ 36 Crostini

1/2 teaspoon seasoned salt

1/2 teaspoon garlic pepper

1/2 teaspoon dried marjoram leaves

1/4 teaspoon ground sage

1-lb pork tenderloin

36 slices (1/4- to 1/2-inch-thick) baguette-style French bread (from 10-oz loaf)

1/4 cup Dijon mustard

3/4 cup apple-cranberry chutney (from 8.5-oz jar)

1/3 cup crumbled blue cheese

Fresh marjoram leaves

1 Heat oven to 425°F. Mix seasoned salt, garlic pepper, marjoram and sage. Rub mixture over pork. Place pork in shallow roasting pan. Insert meat thermometer so tip is in thickest part of pork. Bake uncovered 20 to 25 minutes or until thermometer reads 155°F. Cover pork with aluminum foil and let stand 10 to 15 minutes until thermometer reads 160°F.

2 Meanwhile, reduce oven temperature to 375°F. Place bread slices in ungreased jelly roll pan, 15 1/2×10 1/2×1 inch. Bake about 5 minutes or until crisp; cool.

3 Cut pork into very thin slices. Spread each bread slice with about 1/4 teaspoon mustard. Top each with a thin slice of pork, 1 teaspoon chutney, about 1/2 teaspoon cheese and marjoram leaves.

1 Crostini: Calories 55 (Calories from Fat 10); Total Fat 1g (Saturated Fat 0g); Cholesterol 10mg; Sodium 140mg; Total Carbohydrate 7g (Dietary Fiber 0g); Protein 4g

Spicy Lemon Shrimp with Basil Mayonnaise

Prep Time: 15 min ▪ Start to Finish: 15 min ▪ About 24 Appetizers

1 tablespoon grated lemon peel

3 tablespoons lemon juice

3/4 teaspoon crushed red pepper

1/2 teaspoon salt

2 cloves garlic, finely chopped

3 tablespoons olive or vegetable oil

1 lb uncooked peeled deveined large shrimp (22 to 25 per lb),
    thawed if frozen

1/2 cup loosely packed fresh basil leaves

1/2 cup mayonnaise or salad dressing

1 Set oven control to broil. Mix lemon peel, lemon juice, red pepper, salt, garlic and 1 tablespoon of the oil in medium glass or plastic bowl. Add shrimp; toss to coat. Spread shrimp in ungreased jelly roll pan, 15 1/2×10 1/2×1 inch. Broil with tops 2 to 3 inches from heat 3 to 5 minutes or until shrimp are pink and firm.

2 Place basil and remaining 2 tablespoons oil in food processor. Cover and process until chopped. Add mayonnaise; cover and process until smooth. Serve shrimp with mayonnaise.

1 Appetizer: Calories 55 (Calories from Fat 45); Total Fat 5g (Saturated Fat 1g); Cholesterol 30mg; Sodium 95mg; Total Carbohydrate 0g (Dietary Fiber 0g); Protein 3g

Blueberry Muffin Shortcakes

Pecan Pie Squares

White Chocolate Cherry Crunch

Key Lime Mini-Tarts

Caramel Pecan Cheesecake Bites

Cinnamon Truffles

Raspberry Truffle Cups

Chocolate Truffle Brownie Cups

Florentine Chocolate Profiterole

Almond-Amaretto Tarts

French Silk Tarts

Dark Chocolate Raspberry Fondue

6

serve-yourself
desserts

Blueberry Muffin Shortcakes

Prep Time: 10 min ▪ Start to Finish: 1 hr 40 min ▪ 9 Servings

1 box (18.25 oz) wild blueberry muffin mix
1/2 cup sour cream
1 egg
3/4 cup water
3 tablespoons vegetable oil
Coarse white sugar, if desired
3 cups sliced strawberries
1 cup fresh blueberries
1/3 cup granulated sugar
1 1/2 cups frozen whipped topping, thawed

1 Heat oven to 425°F. Grease or spray bottom and sides of 9-inch square pan.

2 Drain blueberries; rinse and set aside. In medium bowl, stir together sour cream and egg; gradually stir in water and oil. Stir in muffin mix just until blended. Gently stir drained blueberries into batter. Spread batter in pan. Sprinkle with coarse sugar.

3 Bake 25 to 29 minutes or until golden brown. Cool completely, about 1 hour. Meanwhile, in medium bowl, stir together strawberries, 1 cup fresh blueberries and 1/3 cup granulated sugar. Refrigerate until ready to serve.

4 Cut shortcake into 9 squares; cut each square diagonally in half. Place 2 halves on each individual plate; top with berries and whipped topping.

1 Serving: Calories 340 (Calories from Fat 110); Total Fat 12g (Saturated Fat 5g); Cholesterol 30mg; Sodium 300mg; Total Carbohydrate 54g (Dietary Fiber 3g); Protein 4g

Pecan Pie Squares

Prep Time: 15 min ▪ Start to Finish: 2 hrs ▪ 60 Squares

Crust

3 cups all-purpose flour
$3/4$ cup butter or margarine, softened
$1/3$ cup sugar
$1/2$ teaspoon salt

Pecan Filling

4 eggs, slightly beaten
$1^{1}/_{2}$ cups sugar
$1^{1}/_{2}$ cups corn syrup
3 tablespoons butter or margarine, melted
$1^{1}/_{2}$ teaspoons vanilla
$2^{1}/_{2}$ cups chopped pecans

1 Heat oven to 350°F. Grease jelly roll pan, $15^{1}/_{2} \times 10^{1}/_{2} \times 1$ inch. Beat flour, butter, sugar and salt in large bowl with electric mixer on low speed until crumbly (mixture will be dry). Press firmly in pan. Bake about 20 minutes or until light golden brown.

2 To make filling, mix all ingredients except pecans in large bowl until well blended. Stir in pecans. Pour filling over baked layer; spread evenly. Bake about 25 minutes or until filling is set. Cool completely, about 1 hour. For squares, cut into 10 rows by 6 rows.

1 Square: Calories 140 (Calories from Fat 65); Total Fat 7g (Saturated Fat 2g); Cholesterol 20mg; Sodium 55mg; Total Carbohydrate 18g (Dietary Fiber 0g); Protein 1g

White Chocolate Cherry Crunch

Prep Time: 15 min ▪ Start to Finish: 1 hr 15 min ▪ About 16 Servings (½ cup each)

2 cups Corn Chex cereal
2 cups tiny fish-shaped pretzels
2 cups dry-roasted peanuts
1 cup miniature marshmallows
1 package (3 oz) dried cherries (²⁄₃ cup)
1 bag (12 oz) white baking chips (2 cups)
¼ cup half-and-half
½ teaspoon almond extract

1 Toss cereal, pretzels, peanuts, marshmallows and cherries in large bowl.

2 Heat baking chips and half-and-half in 2-quart saucepan over low heat, stirring frequently, until chips are melted. Stir in almond extract.

3 Pour melted mixture over dry ingredients. Toss gently until dry ingredients are coated. Drop mixture by tablespoonfuls onto waxed paper. Let stand about 1 hour or until set. Store loosely covered up to 1 week.

1 Serving: Calories 70 (Calories from Fat 35); Total Fat 4g (Saturated Fat 1g); Cholesterol 0mg; Sodium 50mg; Total Carbohydrate 8g (Dietary Fiber 1g); Protein 2g

Key Lime Mini-Tarts

Prep Time: 10 min ▪ Start to Finish: 1 hr 10 min ▪ 60 Mini-Tarts

1 can (14 oz) sweetened condensed milk
½ cup Key lime juice
1 container (8 oz) frozen whipped topping, thawed
4 packages (2.1 oz each) frozen mini fillo dough shells
Raspberries, if desired

1 Beat milk and lime juice in large bowl with electric mixer on medium speed until smooth and thickened. Fold in whipped topping.

2 Spoon heaping teaspoonful lime mixture into each fillo shell. Cover and refrigerate tarts at least 1 hour or until set but no longer than 24 hours. Garnish with raspberries.

If you don't have Key lime juice, just substitute ½ cup of regular lime juice. You'll need about 2 limes.

1 Mini-Tart: Calories 45 (Calories from Fat 10); Total Fat 1g (Saturated Fat 1g); Cholesterol 5mg; Sodium 25mg; Total Carbohydrate 8g (Dietary Fiber 0g); Protein 1g

Caramel Pecan Cheesecake Bites

Prep Time: 15 min ▪ Start to Finish: 3 hrs 30 min ▪ 70 Bites

Graham Cracker Crust

1 1/2 cups graham cracker crumbs

1/4 cup sugar

1/4 cup butter or margarine, melted

Cheesecake Bites

3 packages (8 oz each) cream cheese, softened

2/3 cup granulated sugar

1 teaspoon vanilla

1/4 cup whipping cream

3 eggs

1/2 cup pecan halves, coarsely chopped

1 tablespoon butter or margarine, softened

1 tablespoon packed brown sugar

1/3 cup caramel topping

1 Heat oven to 325°F. To make the crust, line rectangular pan, 15 1/2×10 1/2×1 inch, with aluminum foil. Mix all ingredients. Press in bottom of pan, using fork. Bake 8 to 10 minutes; cool.

2 Beat cream cheese in large bowl with electric mixer on medium speed until smooth. Gradually beat in granulated sugar and the vanilla until smooth. Beat in whipping cream. Beat in eggs, one at a time. Pour over crust. Stir pecans, butter, brown sugar and caramel topping until mixed; drop evenly over cheesecake.

3 Bake 30 to 35 minutes or until set and light golden brown around edges. Let stand 30 minutes to cool. Cover and refrigerate at least 2 hours but no longer than 48 hours. Cut cheesecake with 1 1/4-inch round cookie cutter; place on serving plate. Drizzle with additional caramel topping if desired.

1 Bite: Calories 95 (Calories from Fat 45); Total Fat 5g (Saturated Fat 3g); Cholesterol 20mg; Sodium 105mg; Total Carbohydrate 11g (Dietary Fiber 0g); Protein 2g

Cinnamon Truffles

Prep Time: 40 min ▪ Start to Finish: 3 hrs 10 min ▪ About 2 dozen Truffles

1 bag (12 oz) semisweet chocolate chips (2 cups)
1 tablespoon butter or margarine
$1/4$ cup whipping cream
1 teaspoon vanilla
$1/2$ teaspoon ground cinnamon
Powdered sugar, if desired
Baking cocoa, if desired

1 Line cookie sheet with aluminum foil or parchment paper. Melt chocolate chips and butter in heavy 2-quart saucepan over low heat, stirring constantly; remove from heat.

2 Stir in whipping cream, vanilla and cinnamon. Refrigerate 30 to 60 minutes, stirring frequently, just until firm enough to roll into balls.

3 Drop mixture by tablespoonfuls onto cookie sheet. Shape into balls. (If mixture is too sticky, refrigerate until firm enough to shape.) Refrigerate about 1 hour until firm.

4 Sprinkle half of the truffles with powdered sugar and half with cocoa. Store in airtight container in refrigerator. Remove truffles from refrigerator about 30 minutes before serving; serve at room temperature.

You may have to keep these under lock and key if you don't want them to disappear before serving!

1 Truffle: Calories 90 (Calories from Fat 55); Total Fat 6g (Saturated Fat 3g); Cholesterol 5mg; Sodium 5mg; Total Carbohydrate 9g (Dietary Fiber 1g); Protein 1g

Raspberry Truffle Cups

Prep Time: 30 min ▪ Start to Finish: 1 hr 35 min ▪ 24 Candies

6 oz vanilla-flavored candy coating (almond bark), cut up
6 oz semisweet baking chocolate, cut up
2 tablespoons butter or margarine, cut into pieces
1/3 cup whipping cream
2 tablespoons raspberry-flavored liqueur or raspberry pancake syrup
24 raspberries

1 Melt candy coating as directed on package. Spread 1 teaspoon coating evenly in bottoms and up sides of 24 miniature paper candy cups. Let stand until hardened.

2 Melt chocolate in heavy 2-quart saucepan over low heat, stirring constantly; remove from heat. Stir in remaining ingredients except raspberries. Refrigerate about 35 minutes, stirring frequently, until mixture is thickened and mounds when dropped from a spoon.

3 Place raspberry in each candy-coated cup. Spoon chocolate mixture into decorating bag with star tip. Pipe mixture into candy-coated cups over raspberry. Place cups on cookie sheet. Refrigerate about 30 minutes or until chocolate mixture is firm. Peel paper from cups before serving if desired. Store tightly covered in refrigerator.

Go wild and whip up two other delectable flavors.
For Cherry Truffle Cups, substitute cherry liqueur for the raspberry liqueur and 24 candied cherry halves for the raspberries. For Crème de Menthe Truffle Cups, add 1/4 cup finely ground almonds to the chocolate mixture and substitute crème de menthe for the raspberry liqueur.

1 Candy: Calories 105 (Calories from Fat 65); Total Fat 7g (Saturated Fat 4g); Cholesterol 5mg; Sodium 15mg; Total Carbohydrate 9g (Dietary Fiber 0g); Protein 1g

Chocolate Truffle Brownie Cups

Prep Time: 15 min ▪ Start to Finish: 1 hr 30 min ▪ 48 Brownie Cups

1 package (19.8 oz) fudge brownie mix
1/4 cup water
1/2 cup vegetable oil
2 eggs
2/3 cup whipping cream
6 oz semisweet baking chocolate, chopped
Chocolate sprinkles, if desired

1 Heat oven to 350°F. Place miniature paper baking cup in each of 48 small muffin cups, 1³/₄×1 inch.

2 Stir brownie mix, water, oil and eggs until well blended. Fill muffin cups about ³/₄ full (about 1 tablespoon each) with batter. Bake 20 to 22 minutes or until toothpick inserted into edge of muffin comes out clean. Cool 10 minutes before removing from pan. Cool completely, about 30 minutes.

3 Heat whipping cream in 1-quart saucepan over low heat just until hot but not boiling; remove from heat. Stir in chocolate until melted. Let stand about 15 minutes or until mixture coats spoon. (It will become firmer the longer it cools.) Spoon about 2 teaspoons chocolate mixture over each brownie. Sprinkle with chocolate sprinkles.

Are you a mint lover? Add 1/2 teaspoon peppermint extract to the brownie batter and sprinkle crushed peppermint candies over the chocolate glaze.

1 Brownie Cup: Calories 80 (Calories from Fat 45); Total Fat 5g (Saturated Fat 2g); Cholesterol 15mg; Sodium 5mg; Total Carbohydrate 9g (Dietary Fiber 1g); Protein 1g

Florentine Chocolate Profiterole

Prep Time: 30 min ▪ Start to Finish: 3 hrs ▪ 6 Servings

1 cup water	2 tablespoons powdered sugar
$^1/_4$ cup butter or margarine	$^1/_2$ teaspoon freshly grated nutmeg
$^1/_2$ teaspoon salt	4 oz semisweet baking chocolate
1 cup all-purpose flour	2 tablespoons water
4 eggs	1 tablespoon honey
1 cup whipping cream	

1 Heat oven to 400°F. Grease and flour cookie sheet.

2 Heat 1 cup water, the butter and salt to rolling boil in 2$^1/_2$-quart saucepan. Stir in flour. Stir vigorously over low heat about 1 minute or until mixture forms a ball. Remove from heat; cool 5 minutes. Beat in eggs, one at a time, until smooth. Drop by rounded tablespoonfuls about 2 inches apart onto cookie sheet.

3 Bake about 30 minutes or until puffed and golden brown. Remove from cookie sheet to wire rack; cool. Cut off tops of puffs; reserve. Pull out any filaments of soft dough from puffs.

4 Beat whipping cream, powdered sugar and nutmeg in chilled medium bowl with electric mixer on high speed until stiff. Fill puffs with whipped cream mixture; replace tops. Mound puffs on large serving plate.

5 Heat remaining ingredients over low heat until smooth; drizzle over puffs. Freeze at least 2 hours until chocolate is firm, or serve immediately. Store covered in refrigerator.

1 Serving: Calories 425 (Calories from Fat 260); Total Fat 29g (Saturated Fat 17g); Cholesterol 205mg; Sodium 310mg; Total Carbohydrate 35g (Dietary Fiber 2g); Protein 8g

Almond-Amaretto Tarts

Prep Time: 40 min   Start to Finish: 2 hrs 15 min   48 Mini Tarts

Pastry

1 cup butter or margarine, softened

1/2 cup granulated sugar

1 egg

1 teaspoon almond extract

2 1/2 cups all-purpose flour

Filling

2 1/4 cups blanched whole almonds

3 eggs

3/4 cup granulated sugar

3 tablespoons amaretto

(or 2 teaspoons almond extract

plus 2 tablespoons water)

2 tablespoons whipping cream

Garnish, if desired

1/2 cup whipping cream

1 tablespoon powdered or

granulated sugar

48 fresh raspberries (about 1 cup)

1 In large bowl, beat butter, 1/2 cup sugar, 1 egg and 1 teaspoon almond extract with electric mixer on medium speed 1 minute. Gradually add flour, beating 1 to 2 minutes just until blended. Cover and refrigerate at least 1 hour until thoroughly chilled.

2 Heat oven to 350°F. Divide pastry into 48 pieces. Gently press pastry onto bottom and side of 48 ungreased mini muffin cups.

3 Place almonds in food processor or blender; cover and process until almonds are finely ground. In medium bowl, mix almonds and remaining filling ingredients with spoon. Spoon about 2 heaping tablespoons filling into each tart crust. Bake 20 to 25 minutes or until golden brown and centers spring back when touched lightly. Cool 5 minutes; gently remove tarts from pan to wire rack. Cool 30 minutes.

4 In chilled small bowl, beat 1/2 cup whipping cream and 1 tablespoon sugar with electric mixer on high speed until soft peaks form.

5 Place 1 teaspoon whipped cream and 1 raspberry on each tart.

1 Mini Tart: Calories 130 (Calories from Fat 70); Total Fat 8g (Saturated Fat 3g); Cholesterol 30mg; Sodium 35mg; Total Carbohydrate 12g (Dietary Fiber 1g); Protein 3g

These tarts freeze well and can be stored in the freezer up to one month. Thaw at room temperature before serving.

French Silk Tarts

Prep Time: 20 min ▪ Start to Finish: 2 hrs 50 min ▪ 16 Tarts

1 box (15 oz) refrigerated pie crusts, softened as directed on box
3 oz unsweetened baking chocolate, cut into pieces
1 cup butter, softened (do not use margarine)
1 cup sugar
1/2 teaspoon vanilla
4 pasteurized eggs* or 1 cup fat-free egg product

1 Heat oven to 425°F. Remove crusts from pouches; unroll on work surface. Pat or roll each crust into 11 1/2-inch circle. With 3 1/2-inch round cutter, cut 8 rounds from each crust; discard scraps. Fit rounds into 16 ungreased regular-size muffin cups, pressing in gently; prick sides and bottom with fork.

2 Bake 7 to 9 minutes or until edges are golden brown. Cool 1 minute; remove from muffin cups to wire rack. Cool completely, about 15 minutes.

3 Meanwhile, in 1-quart saucepan, melt chocolate over low heat; cool. In small bowl, beat butter with electric mixer on medium speed until fluffy. Gradually beat in sugar until light and fluffy. Beat in cooled chocolate and vanilla until well blended. Add eggs, one at a time, beating on high speed 2 minutes after each addition; beat until mixture is smooth and fluffy.

4 Fill tart shells with chocolate mixture. Refrigerate at least 2 hours before serving. Store in refrigerator.

*Because the eggs in this recipe are not cooked, pasteurized eggs must be used. Pasteurization eliminates Salmonella and other bacteria; using regular eggs in this recipe would not be food safe.

1 Tart: Calories 280 (Calories from Fat 180); Total Fat 20g (Saturated Fat 11g); Cholesterol 85mg; Sodium 170mg; Total Carbohydrate 22g (Dietary Fiber 0g); Protein 2g

Dark Chocolate Raspberry Fondue

Prep Time: 20 min ▪ Start to Finish: 20 min ▪ 16 Servings (2 tablespoons each)

²/₃ cup whipping cream
¹/₃ cup seedless raspberry preserves
1 tablespoon honey
1 bag (12 oz) semisweet chocolate chunks
Assorted dippers (fresh fruit pieces, pretzels, shortbread cookies,
    pound cake cubes or angel food cake cubes), if desired

1 Mix whipping cream, raspberry preserves and honey in fondue pot or 2-quart saucepan. Heat over warm/simmer setting or medium-low heat, stirring occasionally, just until bubbles rise to surface (do not boil).

2 Add chocolate; stir with wire whisk until melted. Keep warm over warm/simmer setting. (If using saucepan, pour into fondue pot and keep warm over warm/simmer setting.) Serve with dippers.

No fondue pot? Just serve the fondue in a shallow bowl
    instead of a fondue pot.

1 Serving: Calories 155 (Calories from Fat 80); Total Fat 9g (Saturated Fat 6g); Cholesterol 10mg; Sodium 10mg; Total Carbohydrate 19g (Dietary Fiber 1g); Protein 1g

Helpful Nutrition and Cooking Information

Recommended intake for a daily diet of 2,000 calories as set by the Food and Drug Administration

Total Fat	Less than 65g
Saturated Fat	Less than 20g
Cholesterol	Less than 300mg
Sodium	Less than 2,400mg
Total Carbohydrate	300g
Dietary Fiber	25g

Calculating Nutrition Information

- The first ingredient is used wherever a choice is given (such as $1/3$ cup sour cream or plain yogurt).

- The first ingredient amount is used wherever a range is given (such as 2 to 3 teaspoons).

- The first serving number was used wherever a range is given (such as 4 to 6 servings).

- "If desired" ingredients and recipe variations were not included (such as sprinkle with brown sugar, if desired).

- Only the amount of a marinade or frying oil that is absorbed by the food during preparation was calculated.

Ingredients Used in Recipe Testing and Nutrition Calculations

- The following ingredients, based on most commonly purchased ingredients, are used unless indicated otherwise:

- large eggs, 2% milk, 80%-lean ground beef, canned chicken broth and vegetable oil spread containing at least 65% fat when margarine is used.

- Solid vegetable shortening (not butter, margarine, or nonstick cooking spray) is used to grease pans.

Equipment Used in Recipe Testing

- Cookware and bakeware without nonstick coatings were used, unless otherwise indicated.

- No dark-colored, black or insulated bakeware was used.

- When a pan is specified, a metal pan was used; a baking dish or pie plate means ovenproof glass was used.

- An electric hand mixer was used for mixing when mixer speeds are specified.

Metric Conversion Guide

VOLUME

U.S. Units	Canadian Metric	Australian Metric
¹/₄ teaspoon	1 mL	1 ml
¹/₂ teaspoon	2 mL	2 ml
1 teaspoon	5 mL	5 ml
1 tablespoon	15 mL	20 ml
¹/₄ cup	50 mL	60 ml
¹/₃ cup	75 mL	80 ml
¹/₂ cup	125 mL	125 ml
²/₃ cup	150 mL	170 ml
³/₄ cup	175 mL	190 ml
1 cup	250 mL	250 ml
1 quart	1 liter	1 liter
1 ¹/₂ quarts	1.5 liters	1.5 liters
2 quarts	2 liters	2 liters
2 ¹/₂ quarts	2.5 liters	2.5 liters
3 quarts	3 liters	3 liters
4 quarts	4 liters	4 liters

WEIGHT

U.S. Units	Canadian Metric	Australian Metric
1 ounce	30 grams	30 grams
2 ounces	55 grams	60 grams
3 ounces	85 grams	90 grams
4 ounces (¹/₄ pound)	115 grams	125 grams
8 ounces (¹/₂ pound)	225 grams	225 grams
16 ounces (1 pound)	455 grams	500 grams
1 pound	455 grams	¹/₂ kilogram

MEASUREMENTS

Inches	Centimeters
1	2.5
2	5.0
3	7.5
4	10.0
5	12.5
6	15.0
7	17.5
8	20.5
9	23.0
10	25.5
11	28.0
12	30.5
13	33.0

TEMPERATURES

Fahrenheit	Celsius
32°	0°
212°	100°
250°	120°
275°	140°
300°	150°
325°	160°
350°	180°
375°	190°
400°	200°
425°	220°
450°	230°
475°	240°
500°	260°

NOTE: The recipes in this cookbook have not been developed or tested using metric measures. When converting recipes to metric, some variations in quality may be noted.

Index

Page numbers in italics indicate illustrations.

Whatever's on the menu, make it easy with *Betty Crocker*

Betty Crocker
chicken
tonight
100 Recipes for the Way You Really Cook

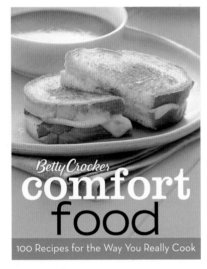

Betty Crocker
comfort
food
100 Recipes for the Way You Really Cook

Betty Crocker
party
food
100 Recipes for the Way You Really Cook

Betty Crocker
quick
fixes
100 Recipes for the Way You Really Cook